THE GAME

written by MICHAEL

ISBN: 0615659209
ISBN-13: 978-0615659206

Many thanks to my lovely editor Lauren.

Wars of the future are wars against ignorance
ineptitude, laziness, and compromise.

This book is dedicated to anyone
unwillingly living a meager existence
to the benefit of those running monopolies.

How much longer will we play the game?

ESSAYS

PREFACE

I didn't want to write a book about politics. I'm much more interested in philosophy; truth in the world. I'm much more interested in the workings of the mind, the body, and the soul. I'm much more interested in the potential of a man; the potential of a woman; the potential of society. I'm infinitely curious about the limits of this one life I have been blessed with.

However, in my attempt to understand the world, understand society, and understand myself, I kept running up against the same wall. I tried to stay away from politics but politics was unwilling to return the favor. And I am not a singular case, or some special exemption. Any who wish to live and let live soon find that they are not left to live themselves.

In trying to understand the boundaries of what is possible in this life—or what could be better—I run up against the same walls. Boundaries have been placed upon our lives and our imaginations and we haven't even realized it. In fact, we're conditioned from birth to never consider the limits of what is possible. We are conditioned to accept the lot we have been given. We're conditioned to consider ourselves lucky or thankful for what we have.

As an example, transportation will never be revolutionized, because the controls on transportation have restricted what is possible, and it has been accomplished by first restricting what is possible in our minds.

Why has nobody made a jetpack? Do you believe we don't have the technology? We can take an organ out of one person and stick it into another! We can't figure out an affordable, efficient way for an individual to fly? First, there would be no way to sell one. It would be regulated out of existence. Established money (and their powerful friends) would market it out of existence. They would conjure some phony science to show how unsafe it is; to scare people into disinterest and disgust. A jetpack would be denied airspace; it would be illegal to fly. Any jetpack would be shot down in the name of safety.

And so people say foolish things like, "Without government, how would we get around?!" When the reality is, *with government* we are all condemned to slow, old technology. Existing systems haven't enabled us to prosper. Existing systems (the monopolies and their friends) have sentenced us to creeping along their roads.

Because of systematic regulations or regulations we have first placed on our own minds; it's simple to dismiss ideas as being *too idealistic,* absolving anyone from having to think or consider anything different—that idealist isn't realistic! That idea is impossible! Except, the world that we live in is a direct result of the cumulative actions of everyone on the planet.

The world isn't a realistic place. We illuminate a room with the flick of a switch. We sit in a seat and fly around the globe. We send a message to somebody on the other side of the planet—thousands of miles away—in less than a second. Consider how many routines of daily life are based on ideas that used to be impossibilities! Impossible only *is* until it *isn't*.

Dismissing the potential for change is unrealistic. Change is happening every second. The world as we know it now is a physical manifestation of the collection of every action of every person on the planet, up to this point. Different actions can create a different result; all of human history is evidence to this point. If we want different actions then we need different ideas. Any popular self-help product is based on changing *thoughts* as a vehicle to changing action. Every person who begins to think and act differently can shift the momentum of the whole in another direction.

I wanted to write a book on ideas and possibilities but I've discovered that we don't need new ideas and new possibilities. Our possibilities are endless. New ideas are everywhere. I've realized that our current situation is not a matter of something new or different; it is a matter of being held in place by existing systems of control. It is a matter of turning imaginations off and destroying spirits, minds, and ultimately, whole societies.

Imagine you went to a dairy farm. Cows litter the tight pens; eating, getting milked, eating, getting milked. Is this the potential of the cow? Is this the beauty of nature, the beauty of life? Is a human any different; cycling between the job, the dinner table, and bed? Is this the fullest expression of life? Is this the potential of man?

And so I'd like to inspire your imagination. I'd like to get us to think of the vastness of existence and the unlimited nature of possibilities. I want to instill confidence in you; we are capable of dealing with each other directly and nonviolently. We are capable of living together in the world. We don't need pens. We don't need the farm. We don't need a farmer. Humans and cows aren't equal, but why would it be acceptable for a human to treat another human like a cow?

We have been blessed with the capacities to create a prosperous, peaceful world for ourselves. We have been blessed with an entire planet. We have been blessed with healthy, functioning minds, bodies, and spirits. Just as the cow lacks nothing to live amongst his fellows in the world, so it is with you and I.

Ultimately, the first step in getting the herd to move outside the fence is disillusionment. They must realize the context of their existence. The truth of our society is that the few with power control the possibilities of the rest. And it's not as if it started from an even footing; the game has been rigged to perpetuate the imbalance of power, indefinitely.

And it's true that this is no utopian idea. There is violence in the wild. There is uncertainty or hardship in the wild. Everything is a trade off. Does the cow want the meal that is provided by the farmer, or does he want his selection from anything available in the natural world? Does he want to walk in relative safety in the pen, or does he want to walk, run, or saunter anywhere he pleases? The cow only has to understand that with each mitigated risk comes a mitigated reward. Aspiring to slavery is the basest of all existence; there is very little risk in being a slave, and there is very little reward.

My goal is to show you—not with statistics, not with personal stories, not with utopian suggestions—that the plantation, the dairy farm, defies the very nature of existence. This book is not focused on statistics, sources, and citations. The statistics are what you can see. The sources are your eyes, your ears, your mind, and your emotions. The citation is our experience as humans in the world. And the purpose of this book is to shatter the myth of reality with observation, critical thought, and principle. This is a book about the observable reality of evil ideas. Not only are we stuck on the farm, but we have become convinced to become active participants in running the farm; at our own expense.

The threat to an established order is new ideas.

The threat to new ideas is an established order.

People are complex. Nature is complex. Societies and governments are complex. Yet, there is an observable, natural order, logic, and the power of the human mind with which we can untangle some of life's mysteries. Almost every day we experience breakthroughs in nutrition, science, and technology.

Various sciences and technologies have advanced at breakneck speeds. 150 years ago, medicine was biting on a stick and sawing off a limb with a hacksaw. Now we can make small incisions with lasers. At the turn of the century, it was a feat to fly across a field. Now we can fly into space. A few decades ago, long distance communication was through letters or phones attached to cables. Now we can send written correspondence instantly, and speak into an untethered piece of plastic and metal to a person on the other side of the planet, in real time.

Advancements are happening at increasing speeds in almost all fields known to man except one: our systems of governance continue to devolve into failure. Our systems of governance all rely on monopolies, chief among these the monopolies of land and violence. We have increasing understanding about the minutia of particles, and seemingly no greater understanding as to the possibilities of non-violently organizing society. Governance hasn't seen a breakthrough in millennia.

Has there ever been a breakthrough in governance? We don't ride horses like the Romans did. We don't fight in legions with swords like the Romans did. In fact, very little of modern life is carried out as it was thousands of years ago. Oral histories have fallen by the wayside; we find information on a computer. Messengers are long gone; we talk to others on phones. Technology has magnified the power of a single person; we fly to destinations in airplanes, bomb countries with unmanned drones, and kill many people with the pull of a trigger.

Unfortunately, there are a few similarities to life thousands of years ago. Most people still consider themselves inferior to the presupposed superiority of the ruling class. Citizens are heavily taxed—for our own good, they would say—as they were thousands of years ago. Citizens allow the ruling class to bully around other nations, devalue their currency, and tell them how to behave—under the threat of injury or death—as they did thousands of years ago.

Politicians have had suspect reputations since the advent of written history, yet they are able to convince the populace that they are acting in the populace's best interest, as they did thousands of years ago. People are forced (or born) into systems of government, as they were thousands of years ago. Elections were rife with fraudulent behavior, as they are today. And despite the entire history of man to the contrary—with few exceptions—people continually allow themselves to be led into destruction by the *good intentions* of their leaders. Governments of old were administered with violence, just as governments today.

With thousands of years of written history at our disposal, we are generally naive about the universal correlation between power and corruption. Until there is a revolution, not in a particular government, but in *governance,* we will continue the legacy of corruption, monopolies, slavery, and destruction that civilizations have been living out since written history began.

We understand the dangers of monopolies in the marketplace. Monopolies are excellent for those who run them and horrific for the consumer. The monopoly can fix the price, ruin the quality, and restrict the supply. And they can do it all without accountability because people cannot take their business elsewhere. The monopoly maintains control over their industry. It seems that, as a society, we understand these ideas.

Then why do we, as a society, tolerate other monopolies; the monopoly on land and violence? Why do we tolerate a monopoly on law? A monopoly on currency? The stakes are even higher. The consequences aren't iPods, the consequences are lives. Everyone seems to be okay with, or unaware, that they will never have free access to land, or that they can be abused or manipulated at any time.

We recognize monopolies are horrible, yet we go beyond tolerating them; we endorse them. Are we aware that we're on the wrong end of monopolies? History has countless lessons of peoples crushed underfoot by monopolies.

In the book, I appear to make metaphorical references to slavery as it existed in the United States 150-200 years ago. It seems metaphorical, but if you see the book through to the end, you'll see that there's very little difference between slavery then and slavery now. Our circumstances seem more humane, but the fundamentals driving slavery are all still very much in place. Slavery was built on a system of monopolies—land, violence, schooling, food, and law—as our current style of governance is built on a series of the same monopolies. It's difficult to name names or point fingers at the particular actors but as the book goes along the picture will be painted clearly.

The slaves are obvious; people who are lorded over while they work for the benefit of the masters. Most citizens of the United States (and people in the world) are slaves. So long as we keep working, pay our taxes, reinforce the powers-that-be; we're free to do whatever we are told. We're free to work when we're told to work. Free to pay taxes when we're commanded. And free to go to jail (or be investigated by secret police organizations) if we disagree. You can have whatever donut you like so long as your masters get their cut off the top.

The Slave Masters are becoming clearer all the time. The political elite. The business elite. The banking elite. The moneyed elite we never hear about. The more research I do, the more I pay attention, the more the same people seem to keep showing up to call the shots of the largest organized crime cartel in the history of the world; from seemingly ordinary bankers to Bohemian Grove to republicans and democrats to Bilderberg.

Overseers are the key. In the current system, they maintain the power of the ruling elite. Overseers buffer the elite from the people. Teachers, government workers, judges, police, military, bankers—anyone who perpetuates monopolies of school, law, enforcement, currency, etc.

Hitler may be the face of Nazism, but tens of thousands of faceless, jackbooted thugs carried out his evil ideas. The President of the United States is obviously an evil man, but it's the thousands of faceless police who fight the illegitimate war on drugs who perpetuate the evil ideas and laws. Or thousands of faceless soldiers who fly overseas to murder undeserving peoples around the globe. Or tens of thousands of tellers, traders, and managers at major financial institutions. The government can have an educational model, but it's the thousands of faceless teachers (themselves already mentally crippled by the institution of school) who are mentally crippling future generations.

The compliance of the everyday man gives evil a free pass. It's the overseers who are responsible for maintaining a system of control, and it's the overseers who will fight to the death to maintain the system that benefits their masters.

There isn't an end to the problems that we face. Human perfection is off the table. However, that doesn't make it acceptable to aspire to—or settle for—shit. The choice is ours and *better* is an option. Some people believe in violence; murder, rape, and theft. As Socrates lamented at the end of "The Republic", the justice-minded man of his ideals could never exist in the politics of his time, or ours. The rewards of politics are money and power; what kind of man desires money and power? Not the kind of many anyone would want to have either... All the more reason why honest individuals must proactively band together for their mutual well-being.

I believe there is a host of my peers in this country—in the world—who do not see their actions as having an impact; they go where popular tides flow. As a result, they are complicit in every choice made by the mob—which can only be bad choices (as you will see later). There is no end to the fools presently clamoring for *democracy,* but Plato wrote thousands of years ago that, "democracy passes into despotism". So the multitude clamors for the consolidation of power and corruption.

> "The key to the age may be this, or that, or the other, as the young orators describe; -- the key to all ages is -- Imbecility; imbecility in the vast majority of men, at all times, and, even in heroes, in all but certain eminent moments; victims of gravity, custom, and fear. This gives force to the strong, -- that the multitude have no habit of self-reliance or original action." -Ralph Waldo Emerson

Combined with the understanding that "ignorance is bliss", it would seem that most people—most Americans—are (unwittingly) satisfied to be used for the whims of the powerful and deranged. Are most people really satisfied with putting the force of their lives behind the murderous forces of states and madmen? History would seem to suggest so. Willful ignorance: fueling the needless slaughter of peaceful neighbors since the dawn of humanity.

I have aspired to write a book that is different than any I have ever read. We live in crazy times and every day that passes is only getting crazier. Each of us has access to more information than possibly all people who have ever lived...combined.

When Socrates, Plato, Aristotle, and Diogenes walked the Earth, they had the full force of human experience at their fingertips, but only a fraction of our accumulated information. As time as gone on, we've acquired libraries full of histories, scientific knowledge, philosophical treatises, literature, and poetry of every kind. Information may have been scarce, difficult to acquire, or unknown at the time, but it required much less time and effort for a man to grasp at least a fraction of human knowledge.

In the present, it would take many lifetimes just to read all that is known; and that before beginning to consider it's application. The struggle *for* knowledge has turned—subtly, without demarcation—into the struggle to make sense and application of what is known. A man honestly in search of the truth can drown before ever reaching sight of land.

This understanding has affected the book in two ways; the most obvious being brevity. I could elaborate on each section of the book—even on each point—as you can read many authors who have written entire books on a single subject or event, but the point isn't elaborate details.

The second affect has been on my view of life. If a man has no way to apply all the information in all the libraries of the world, how useful is the information? It is not enough to merely *have information,* a man also needs a way to *apply* the information. Without a better means of application, much of our accumulated information amounts to nothing.

Many contemporary writers are focused on writing detailed accounts of various corruptions in government and society. There are many new accounts of historical events that shatter old myths and shed new truths. Except, without a means of application, the new truth is wasted. Each revealed corruption is another banana peel tossed onto a landfill. This isn't to say that those researchers and writers are wasting their time; only to say that I think they do a thankless job, and the information has to be applied. What are we supposed to do with the new information?

In general, history has been written and the minds of men are made up. Past truths influence minds in the present (and future) but what has all this revealing of truth brought us? Revealing the truth in details only steers the ship slightly over the course of generations. Without principle, even truths uncovered in the present time (such as our government's new abilities to legally detain American citizens via the NDAA) are only negligible at best. Unfortunately, speaking truth to power is only a single step in a marathon. By the time truth can be spoken, heard, and understood, generations have perished. We will all be long dead—after a lifetime of slavery—before truth is properly spoken to the evil powers of our time. We will be long dead before our generation can be convinced as to the truth of every detail of the present. The only action pertinent enough to make a difference in our lifetime is principled living. Principled living is the tool to apply knowledge and truth; wherever you are, however you can, whenever you have the time—principled living, against the whims of mobs; in the face of illimitable power.

If a man can be convinced to live on principle, no amount of historical correction is necessary because very little of human history is necessary. Whether Lincoln was a humanitarian—freer of the slaves—or whether he was a horrible tyrant—destroyer of states-rights and 600,000 of his own citizens—has little impact on the man of principle today. The truth is useful—as all truth is—in informing the man of principle about reality, but the man of principle is busy living; busy making his own history. The man of principle doesn't vacation to historical sites; wherever he is is a historical site. The man of principle—as demonstrated by principled men of past—writes history as he goes.

Principled living isn't about rigidity for the sake of rigidity. Principled living is about living according to what is true and real. We all understand and behave as if gravity is universal and real. Is murder not so universal? Is it not so real? Isn't aggressive violence as easy to define as gravity? The behavior of men does not seem as certain about murder as it is about gravity. If violence is universal, real, and wrong, shouldn't our behavior reflect this truth?

The principled man makes an honest effort to discover and understand the principle. Principled living is an unceasing search for whatever is excellent, true, and real. This is where those detectives of the truth come in; informing reality. It isn't the man with the most truth, or the man with the most rigidity who is the most principled, but the man who is most motivated to see the journey through to the end. I imagine every good and true conclusion that can be reasoned will be reached by any who are limitlessly motivated. Honest motivation goes the distance. Thoreau put it poetically, "In the long run, men hit only what they aim at."

It is obvious that we need more principled men and women. However, it is also obvious that the deck is stacked against principles. A mighty system of slavery and monopolies looms. Minds and emotions are crushed before they can flower in full. People are manipulated against each other. The world can seem large and depressing. But all anyone need do is look at the target in the distance they wish to hit and continually do what they can, where they are at, with what they have. With each person who discovers original thought and action, the mass has one less bit of momentum hurdling itself toward the cliff.

Limits of possibility begin by being self-imposed, leading to limits on humanity being systematically imposed. The systems we currently live in stifle our imaginations first and our reality last. And so I write with three goals; shattering the illusion of the system, setting loose your imagination, and inspiring your participation in your own destiny. I believe most people do not realize they are pouring their lives down the drain to reinforce a system of monopolies and violence and these people cannot possibly change course until they are aware. I write with the hopes of using our experience as humans, observations about the natural world, and simplistic logic as a basis for articulating a complaint, not with Bush, not with Obama, but with the system of monopolies and violence in place that allows for a Bush, an Obama, and billions of trampled people, worldwide. A system that allows for extortion, coercion, homelessness, starvation, theft, rape and murder. A system that perpetuates the exploitation of, not just the third world, not just developing countries, but almost all of humanity. A system of slavery.

Revolutions of the future are not taking place on battlefields. Revolutions of the future (if there is to be any revolutions of the future) will have to take place in the minds and hearts of men and women. Only when minds and hearts are convinced to abandon the current system—the current way of thinking—will human society decide on a new venture; one in which a picture of the future is not "imagine a boot stamping on a human face — forever." as it is in "1984"; as it is now becoming. We are entering a dystopian age—not because of systems—but because of dystopian dreams and ideals in the hearts and minds of men, and their legion of ignorant followers.

Anyone can google outer space and look at immense images of the universe. It is simple to see possibilities in the neighbor's yard just as easily as it is to see possibilities in the vastness of space. However, space is wrongly called the final frontier. The final frontier, the place few have been yet willing to visit, is the vast inner reaches of the mind and heart. No man or woman who has ever lived has seen past the horizon of their own potential; there is no end. If we are going to go anywhere in the world, we must first go somewhere within ourselves.

The revolutions of the future are not about free markets or non-violent governments. The revolutions of the future are about free markets minds and non-violent hearts. When minds and hearts are thoroughly convinced of what is right and true, when imaginations are unleashed, when each one does what he can; only then will we have systematic revolution.

INTERNAL CONTROL

The following essays are all centered on ways that our nature is taken advantage of; internal control. Various methods of internal control are fundamental; once a mind is put into a wheelchair, the body follows. Not literally, of course, but in every way that counts. Those in power don't worry about controlling information if a person can be convinced to not bother thinking in the first place, or if they can spend all their extra time entertained, or if they can be made to not care at all. And so much of our society on the surface—I think of it as The American Dreamworld—works to keep the average American locked inside of their own head and emotions, entertained into submission, and fighting other Americans. The following pages detail how you get trapped within yourself.

HUMAN NATURE

Two hundred and fifty years ago Rousseau wrote, "Man is born free, and everywhere he is in chains." Sadly, nothing has changed. Our chains begin within; we are trapped inside by a faulty nature. There are so many negative defaults: anger, jealousy, lust, laziness, gluttony, greed... All have applied to me at one point or another (and will again soon, no doubt). Everyone struggles.

Human nature—our default behaviors—is the race we cannot outrun. We've been given a brain, capable of reasoning, but it often seems a feeble tool in the face of our inner desires. The brain can seem like a massive force, but it is easily swept aside when it confronts our inner nature.

In fact, much of our brain's development happens in the direction of our nature. Do you want to be rich? You're going to figure out how to make it happen. Do you want to be lazy? Your brain will solve that problem. Do you really want to do that thing your brain tells you not to do? Your brain will figure out a way to make that work too, in spite of it's best objections.

Despite the best attempts at logic (all of which I am firmly in favor of), we still have not found a way to outrun, out gun, or outsmart our innermost insides. Alcoholics, murderers, rapists, thieves, and the slovenly were all around thousands of years ago. We've got our own crop of these characters running around today. Their mere existence is a testament to a warped quality inside of us. We can eradicate diseases. We haven't yet eradicated laziness. If anything, laziness is as alive and well as ever.

In these writings, this is probably where I could just end early. If there's no fixing human nature, why go on?

Human nature is the rock on which all other corruption is built; the corruption from within. Outside systems cannot be addressed without considering the innate, imperfect qualities of the people who built them.

It's a catch-22. Human nature can never be overcome, at least by human means. Yet, it makes no sense to just sit by and let the best of the worst in us run amuck.

Outside of a spiritual transformation, our minds can aid us in the mitigation of our own nature; we still have brains. In spite of our overpowering nature, our brains can help us work toward improving our actions. Awareness of a better action is the first step toward making a better decision. It's not a solution, it's not perfection, but it can be a tool to help us.

A perfect system is not the point. Perfection is never an option but that doesn't mean we have to settle for where we are at. What excuse do we have for not attempting to do better? The purpose of perfection, or ideals; they give us a direction to head. We can understand ideals with our minds and strive for them with our actions.

The mind can become one of our greatest allies, or one of our greatest threats. The mind can be developed into a weapon of powerful force. Your mind can take you past the borders of the known world. Or it can atrophy into retardation and weakness, dragging your entire life down with it.

The host of people who made fortunes on real estate in the early 2000's didn't figure that they needed to understand much about law, governance, currency, or economics. But when many of them got foreclosed on in droves—lives now crushed under a loss of assets and ruined credit—they probably now wish they understood how the world was working ahead of time.

Ignorance is only bliss until you are crushed by what you didn't know.

BASIC NECESSITY

I've worked on a golf course, a sporting goods store, a temp office, a Pizza Hut, Starbucks (twice), worked for a moving company, sold cars at a Toyota dealership, sold cell phones at Verizon (a hundred times more unethical than selling cars), worked at a drug store, stocked shelves overnight at Target, cleaned a rich man's house weekly, done data entry over the internet, babysat, mowed yards, and a few other things. I'm no stranger to work. Strangely, I've done all that work and now have very little to show for it. Outside of a computer, some books, and a few other things, where did all of my work go?

(Minus what I squandered on petty crap..) I ate it. I drank it. I slept under a roof. And I'm wearing some of it.

Necessities, as their name indicates, are unavoidable. I have to eat and drink. I need a shelter from the elements. A home is nourishing, not only to my body, but mind and soul. I have to put clothes on to go out into the world.

Acquiring these resources should be synonymous with living, since living is impossible without them. There are three ways to acquire the resources needed to survive:

We can work for resources and/or trade them on the market; *labor.* We can plow the land, cultivate the fruit, gather the water, and build the shelter. We create sustenance with our labor.

The second way we can acquire resources is to have them given to us; *gifts.* Resources can be gifted to us from another or even from nature. Depending on the circumstance, the fruit tree can be a gift of nature, or a work of labor.

Beyond receiving or creating, the only option left is to pilfer. *Theft.* We can take resources from our neighbors by force.

All of our necessities, all of the resources we require to continue living, come from the Earth; from the land. Uses of the term "self-reliance" are often associated directly with farming, cultivating the land, creating your own tools, and harvesting your own resources because the ultimate source of the resources required to survive come from land. How can a person get the things to survive without having access (directly or indirectly—the market) to land?

Those who never have direct access to land are rarely able to create a fruitful living for themselves unless they create surplus (money, goods) to exchange on the market. How many tenants are wealthy compared with landlords?

If you cannot grow your own food, you will have to buy it. If you cannot make clothes, you will have to buy them. Your existence is reliant on your being able to exchange in the market for the necessities you cannot produce. It's not a problem if somebody would *choose* to make a living without land, the evil is in being *forced*. The evil is in a system that leaves so many landless; cut off from the means of life.

It's no wonder that we live in a system of violence. It's no wonder that our work will never seem to be over. It's no wonder that few prosper while many work themselves to exhaustion. How can you prosper when you will never control the means of your own life? We are born into this society, into this method of societies around the world, into being cut off from our birthright before we take a single breath.

There's a lot of talk around having the *right to life,* but I rarely hear a whisper as to the right to *sustain* your own life. Everyone has a scheme for controlling the land and doling it out "fairly". Absurd! We should start imagining a world where the *right to life* goes right along with the *right to sustain your own life* by means of finding your own place in the land. It's a difficult solution to imagine. Especially difficult if you're attempting to live high atop a system of monopolies.

Whomever created the Earth should be the one to hold dominion. How can one man—a group of men or, God forbid, a corporation—rope off an area that humanity and nature are no longer allowed to touch? On what grounds can a group of men cut off the birthright of humanity? Don't we all have an equal claim?

SELF-INTEREST

There isn't a single person on the planet who isn't (at least a little) self-interested. In a general sense, it is natural for people act in their own self interest. If you don't eat, you don't keep living, so you've got to do something to make sure you can keep putting food in your mouth.

Anyone a hair more self-interested than you is called *greedy.* Greed may be the root of the absolute corruptibility of power. At some point, with some amount of power, it is sure to be abused. The tricky part of greed is that it never ends; it is only focused on *more.* There is no limit; always *more.*

Greed—overabundant self-interest—is a problem of it's own, but I think we can come to some simple understandings; understandings which should lead us to behave in particular ways, *by default.* The general lack of this default behavior is evidence of non-existent understanding.

If we understand that everyone is going to operate in their own self-interest, why would we want to design—or support a societal structure—where certain people are going to have clear opportunities to take advantage of others? The average person understands that we don't want "bad guys" to have nuclear weapons. But if we think about it for a moment, why would we want *anyone* to have nuclear weapons? Sure, "good guys" are "capable" (key word) of acting in the name of the "greater good" (abstractly relative measurement, or anyone not being blown to bits), but they're *certain* to act in their own interest. The self-interest of politicians is always conveniently aligned with the "greater good" or "general welfare" (until proven otherwise, as it often is).

I don't blame politicians for shady business. It's deplorable, of course, but they should never be put in a situation where they can scheme with little-to-no-recourse at the expense of the people they are supposed to be representing. The system allows for an ever increasing amount of corruption—under the guise of good intentions with the aid of emotional manipulation—and the citizenry, by and large, goes right along.

If we understood that people will always act in their own self interest, we would rarely—if ever—accede to a power increase for the powerful.

On a societal level, a mitigating factor of one's self-interest is the self-interest of another; competing self-interests. Two people competing for the same ends keeps both of them somewhat in check. Sports are a great example; two sides competing—in a theoretically neutral environment—toward the same goal. When the playing field is even, each side provides resistance to the other. Unfortunately, the rest of life is not so even a playing field. Notice how world powers (those with nuclear weapons) do not openly pick fights with other world powers (those with nuclear weapons), only with those who do not. Thanks to Gaddafi, countries now see the foolishness of disarming themselves in the face of an even greater power. We all would be wise to learn the same lesson.

Life being an uneven playing field means that those beginning with a disadvantage should take greater care in playing. The first rule of thumb should be to never acquiesce greater power to those who already have more power (than you). They're going to act in their self-interest, as you or I would. Who is more likely to come out on top in an issue of conflicting interests?

This is evidenced in mammoth corporations who give the finger to various local communities or foreign countries. They're not acting under altruistic ideals; they're out to make money. They do as much as they can get away with and (maybe) ask forgiveness later (or quietly settle out of court). If we were really concerned about the power of large companies—and keeping local resources pooled locally—we would stop supporting multinational corporations; producing and consuming locally (as much as possible). Large corporations are only acting in their own self-interest, but they have become so successful by convincing millions of people to stop acting in their self-interest, or in the interest of their community.

Another strong mitigating factor to self-interest is moral hazard. Moral hazard is essentially consequences; living in a world where the danger of facing them is real. If a person is allowed to face the consequences of their actions, their behavior will either be limited, or they will face the consequences. Why don't most people go walking out onto the freeway? The consequences of walking on a freeway are real.

An understanding of self-interest would have us work toward leveling the playing field with a system that allows as much competition and moral hazard as possible. Any system designed to control the self-interest of others—especially by a few at the expense of many—will only lead to an abuse of the system by the few. The few are just as self-interested as everyone else.

Are there any examples of a person giving up power and money for principled reasons? They are few and far between. So few and far, that it's safe to assume the opposite. Power is rarely given up...except by the individual with little to spare. Individuals, under a little duress, hardship, or ignorance, will gladly relinquish their power for the promise of relief.

The general understanding of self-interest in our society has been destroyed. We believe in the altruistic intentions of politicians. We believe some people (even non-religious people) have a holy, selfless bend. We don't believe that people will simply get a piece for themselves—even though the government, and every professional industry, is filled with countless examples to the contrary.

When people are put into situations where they can get something for themselves, they most likely do so. The greater the gain, the more likely they are to act in their own interest.

There are many at the top, gaming the system. Many brainwashed enforcers of the system. Many at the bottom, aware that they are being taken advantage of, but unable to articulate a complaint; crushed none-the-less. The only real way to move the system in a good direction is to *remove the imbalances*. Systematic problems will disappear in correlation with the dismantling of the system.

With every mention of a removing of some system in society, there are always the armchair humanitarians who cry about some demographic; soon to be bleeding in the streets. The reality is that there will always be poor, abused people. But the reality doesn't have to be that poor people stay poor and abused. Systems of "regulation", control, and redistribution only ensure the poverty and abuse for generations. Only when we agree to remove all restraints —restraints which have allowed the rich to ride on the back of the rest—will we actually see how high and far each man can fly.

When big banks make bad decisions and go bankrupt, other banks are less inclined to behave foolishly. Risk and consequences create accountability and more responsible behavior. The lack of regulations would allow more banks to compete. On the flip side, when big banks get bailed out, all banks are more inclined to behave foolishly. A lack of risk and consequences encourages greed. Regulations create a cartel of crooked bankers.

When government makes decisions that are harmful to citizens, and citizens continue to support it, government feels free to make more harmful decisions. When citizens don't put up with crap from the government, government is less likely to make harmful decisions.

Yet, we continue to promote systems where self-interested people are put into positions of monopolized power, at the expense of the populace. At what point will the average citizen realize that allowing *any* other person so much power is foolish?

Systems that allow one person to fulfill their self-interest at the expense of others will *always* be abused. I am not aware of a single example to serve as the exception to the rule. The larger the system, the more greed is allowable; greater corruption is assured. The larger the system, the more people involved; the more victims of corruption.

ACCOUNTABILITY

If you've ever driven in a city—usually stop and go around 20mph—you'll notice plenty of pedestrians walking across the street, whether they have the walk sign or not. Plenty of people have no reservation about running out in front of traffic if they're in a hurry.

Cars and trucks rip down the freeway at speeds of 60 mph, or faster. I'm not sure I have ever seen anyone run across several lanes of traffic on a freeway. Freeways might be a little out of the way of the average pedestrian, but I've driven down plenty of high-speed highways in cities and pedestrians are always waiting patiently while traffic rushes past at 45mph or faster. Pedestrians seem to be in much less of a hurry when the traffic is going much faster. Why? Accountability.

We're told that accountability is the Constitution, some sort of law, regulations, or elections. A few lies among many. The general populace will be forever chasing a non-existent idea of accountability when it comes to politicians, banksters, or corporations, because real accountability is only found in one place; consequences.

Let's say I wrote a law. Rather, one of my friends in business helped me write a law. A few other friends are responsible for enforcing the law and ruling on the law that I wrote. Other than altruistic conjecture, what is my motivation to obey the law? Or, better yet, I'll just write the law to work around whatever behaviors I wish to engage in. Then I (and my friends) can maintain the visage of obeying the law while others suffer for similar, yet not exact, behavior.

It's naive to imagine we live in a world where people in power behave according to some sort of stated accountability when they do not face the consequences of their actions. Given the power to steal and murder, we're just supposed to take everyone at their word that they'd never do such a thing; even though there are millions of examples of people who go to much further lengths to accomplish these sordid crimes. Eddie Murphy shows the system at work in *The Distinguished Gentleman.*

Would you play a sport against another team if they designed the field, created the rules, and supplied the referees? Yet when companies (help) write legislation, politicians sign it, their mutual friends (in some cases, the same people) in "regulatory agencies" approve the (questionable) products, and their other friends are in charge of enforcing the laws, we are all supposed to believe that altruistic accountability has taken place. A pony-show is more important than legitimate accountability, if you can maintain an ignorant population.

If we want accountability, businesses have to be allowed to go out of business. Laws have to be applied universally; or not at all. Banks who took terrible risks would have to be allowed to fail. Everyone would be equally at risk of suffering the consequences of their actions. Evil, stupid people would pay the price for being evil and stupid.

And if they don't—if the system is rigged to prevent the powerful from suffering the consequences of their own actions—then somebody else has to suffer. The somebody else is taxpayers, victims, those caught in legal loopholes, and the occasional patsy; tossed under the bus to maintain the illusion.

That's why you never see pedestrians run across the freeway. A semi-truck speeding down the freeway deals with kings and peasants equally; all are held accountable for mistakes and stupidity.

MIND CONTROL

Indecision is death. To live is to do. It is to love, to hope, to want, to try, to dare, to risk, to fail, to build, to destroy, to make a mistake, to get angry and do something about it.

Living is messy. In order to have any opinion, you must feel and you must choose. Some may wish to avoid any conflict, avoid disturbance, avoid risk, or avoid pain. Some are unable to make up their mind and heart about two positive outcomes. Indecision is one of the saddest experiences to witness. The inability to choose is the inability to live. What is life, but a series of choices?

One of the foremost tools in choosing is the mind. Our minds are fragile. They are easily influenced by a variety of forces we often don't consider; the most formidable of these forces is our emotions. Our emotions can turn the screws on anything happening inside of our brains. A manipulation of one (our brain or our emotions) ends up being a manipulation of both, and the manipulation of a person entirely.

Our brains are also weakened by what we already know. This is called *confirmation bias.* We are likely to search out information, or skew all incoming information, to reinforce what we already know. We're more likely to gravitate toward that news station that reports the news with a slant you already agree with. We're more likely to read books with conclusions you already endorse. Even in writing this book from an unconventional viewpoint, I am at a serious disadvantage. Your mind is almost certain to be predisposed against an unknown view.

Though it cannot overpower your emotions, your brain can have a tremendous influence on the way your emotions are formed and executed. Your brain is your first line of defense against the manipulation of your brain and emotions, or the first weapon used against your brain and emotions; this is why slavery begins in the mind.

Centuries ago, slavery seemed like a purely physical ordeal. People were put to work under the direct threat of violence and death. The reality was a vast psychological component of slavery that has increased as time has gone on. Direct violence is not as necessary (but still useful) to maintain the institution of slavery in present times due to massively powerful means of mental and emotional manipulation. Technology has advanced, wealth has accumulated, and the techniques of the slave masters have become more advanced. Those unaware have been painted into a corner; it is extremely difficult for a person to attain dominion over their own mind.

Media incessantly blasting. Opinions are flying thick through the air. Advertising everywhere. Everything in small clips and snippets. Loudness! It's difficult to sift through the noise to discover any authentic information. Lies. Half-truths. Misinformation. Obfuscation. Mandatory schooling. It almost always requires a conscious effort to begin to hear yourself think.

Mind control begins by controlling input. Out of sight, out of mind. If your mind is unaware of an idea, controlling interests will never have to debate the merits of the idea. Notice that government itself never debates the idea of government being a monopoly. So long as the issue is never brought up, it never needs to be addressed. Since it is never brought up, people live with the assumption that government *will* be a monopoly. The battle of ideas is won without a shot fired.

It is difficult to think of something you have never thought of before. If you cannot think of the ways in which you are controlled, how will you ever realize your constraints? How will you ever resist them?

When we are told, "There are two certainties in life: death and taxes." and believe it, we only end up ensnaring our own minds. We take something finite and limited (taxes) and make it an absolute that is not able to be worked around or lived without. The hurdle begins in the mind. Slavery begins in the mind.

Every limit placed on your mind becomes a limit placed on your life. Every hurdle placed into our lives by crooked governments begins with hurdles placed on our minds and, even deeper, emotions.

INTELLECTUAL SLOTH

Dam it up. Divert it. Bottle it up. Water can be affected in many ways but it always does two things; it takes the shape of it's container and it follows the path of least resistance. We have a lot in common with water.

Conformity isn't an absolute but it's certainly a strong urge. We want to be accepted. We want to be liked. We want to fit in. We're social creatures. We want to be part of the group.

I couldn't say for certain whether true individuals are born or created, but I think it's some combination of both. Regardless, we have a propensity to behave as part of the group. It is easy to go along with the herd. It is easy to float downstream.

If there's one thing we like, it's easy. Easy is the quickest payoff. Easy is the least effort. Easy is the least risk. Easy is the easiest to rationalize. You can't shut a brain down, but you can make it move on, move downstream, to more trivial matters with a solid rationalization.

There's one rationalization, the king of rationalizations, that destroys all thought everywhere. This rationalization can pacify entire generations. This rationalization can paralyze entire nations. This rationalization can blow your brain out of your skull and into the wind.

As soon as a person believes, as soon as a person settles on, as soon as a person thinks this one thought; action is unnecessary, boundaries are clearly seen, brains melt away, men become cattle, possibilities are over, skies have limits, odds become statistics, life loses meaning, and the future is only a formality:

That's just the way it is.

ILLUSORY CHEESE, SENTIMENTAL INVESTMENT, AND THE EMOTIONAL FORTRESS

The mind is an easy place to get trapped. Trapped due to outside pressures. Trapped due external circumstances. Or trapped due to emotional anchoring. There are a few principles in the way the mind works that, when taken advantage of, that can turn a mind into it's own greatest enemy. The people who run monopolies understand how minds work; the system is set up to encourage us to use our minds against ourselves.

A common technique is akin to turning the mind into a maze—setting you loose like a mouse—with the goal of finding the cheese (that, unbeknownst to you, doesn't exist; illusory cheese).

The false objective is the illusory cheese. The cheese doesn't exist, but the mouse runs around in the maze anyhow. So long as the mouse is looking for the cheese—kept busy on an invisible problem—the mouse will never consider the reality (and futility) of running around the maze.

False objectives are easy to understand, but people still get caught looking for them. Gay Marriage—on the Federal level in particular—is illusory cheese. There is no Federal solution. There is no cheese. In fact, it is the Federal Government's involvement that causes the issue to be a problem in the first place. There is no single Federal solution for 300 million people; the only possible solution is for the Federal government to relinquish all authority over marriage. Strangely, nobody ever asks what authority government has over marriage—or why they should—only that government should do this or that. It's a fantasy issue, designed to keep people looking for it (or fighting over it) in the maze, distracted from real issues; the creation of a police state or the Federal Reserve daily despoiling the populace.

The false parameters that arise from the illusory cheese are just as fantastical as the non-existent objective. Many people are caught up in this party or that party, but they're unable to see that the entire method of solving the problem is false because there is no real objective that they can arrive at. There is no democrat or republican ideal or solution they are aiming at. The parties are split between two abstract, relative terms; conservative and liberal. Party lines are false parameters; as real as invisible cheese. Neither side has any sort of "solution", yet both sides keep people busy while any conclusions from the issue will only further the government's own power. Gay marriage should be irrelevant but it has come into the political forefront to distract and ensnare minds that might otherwise wander onto real issues of monopolization, murder, slavery, and theft.

Illusory cheese is a powerful tool of the slave master. We are tempted with illusory cheese a thousand times over in daily life. Turn on any political news network and they'll be addressing the same issues that they were addressing last year, five years ago, and fifty years ago. How can these same problems still exist?

Some of the problems are very real. However, we get presented with (typically) two illusory solutions (a republican solution and a democrat solution) that never solve the problem. The never solve the problem because the system that facilitates democrats and republicans is what is causing the problem. Regardless of which choice you select, people will continue to suffer as they did before, while the people who made money will continue making the money as they have been. If you can be kept fixated on illusory solutions—illusory cheese—you'll never address the real issue. The mastery of illusion becomes the mastery of reality.

The economy is a great example. Republicans will present you with their opinions about why the economy is failing and condemn the democrats. Democrats present you with theirs and condemn the republicans. Neither party's solutions will actually ever do anything about the economy, since neither addresses the real problems (the monopoly of central banking, enforced by a monopoly on violence), so whichever side of the fence you fall on is fine with the people in power—the people siphoning wealth upward. The problem perpetuates. People in power stay in power (or increase in power). The people in control don't really care what side you choose, since they're two phony choices. All that matters is that you choose one of the phony choices (or better, bicker about it with some other sucker) so the game can go on as it has. The same people in power, making money. The same people taken advantage of by the system. Illusory cheese.

An even more powerful way we get trapped is building up an emotional fortress around our decisions. I call it *sentimental investment.*

After making a decision—as time passes—we develop an emotional tie to our decision. We become attached to the decision. It becomes a part of our identity. We make other decisions based on the decision that we've already made. The emotions we attach to the decision build up over time—sentimentally—into a fortress of emotions around the original decision. Any evidence for a new decision must be strong enough to overcome the emotional fortress we have created around the original decision.

Emotions themselves are not intrinsically good or bad but emotions are certainly a much stronger driver of human behavior than reason. Due to the conflicting nature of reason and emotions inside of us—at the time of decision making—emotions can often hinder us from making a reasonable decision. The investment is sentimental because it is emotion stored up positively over time, even positive reinforcement from a negative situation.

The emotional fortress often clouds—if not directly opposes—our ability to come to a logical decision. "Love is blind" because an emotional fortress surrounds the feelings and thoughts of another. We understand the idea when applied to love, but it also applies to any other decisions. If you believe yourself to be a democrat, and you have a negative experience with a republican, your positive feelings about democrats—the people who agree with you—will be reinforced positively. Political parties make a special effort toward emotional manipulation.

Let's say I go to the store to buy a pair of shoes. I could spend my time searching for the best deal, trying on all the top pairs, doing research into the best quality, and so on. Let's say I do a thorough, rational search to find the right pair and buy them. As I wear them I'll get some nice memories in the shoes. People will complement my shoes. I'll think I look good in them. I'll feel good in the shoes. I might discover that a professional athlete or celebrity also wears these shoes (if I hadn't before I bought them) and a high profile endorsement reinforces my good feelings. My shoes say that I'm stylish, or tough, or sporty.

Once the shoes are worn out, what will I do? Confirmation bias says that I'll go looking for similar shoes. Instead, let's say I want to be thorough, so I do the entire shop around a second time. I look at reviews, inspect quality, try on a variety of pairs. However, I still have an emotional fortress built up around the previous shoes.

For me to make a different purchasing decision, the logical reasons for making the new decision must overcome my emotional ties to the previous shoes. If a rival brand of shoes is the same price, similar quality, similar look, and similar feel then they know I'm going to go with the old brand. This is why price becomes such a competitive fixture; they have no other options. The new brand competing for my business cannot likely connect with me emotionally in a way that will overcome the emotional ties that I've already built up with the old brand. This is why companies hire celebrities and spokespeople for us to identify emotionally with. They hope our emotional desire to "be like Mike" will outweigh any rational decision to the contrary.

Companies spend millions of dollars helping us build emotional fortresses around their products. They flood television with relentless advertising so it seems they are a *popular* brand. We'll fit in with the crowd and be accepted. Then they tailor their advertising to say that we'll be real individuals, we'll be special, if we buy their shoes. Double whammy. You get to fit in with the crowd and be special at the same time. (I'm not sure how it's possible to be an individual and part of the group simultaneously. Popular culture challenges each individual to the impossible task of being simultaneously popular and unique. Let's just say it's better if we don't think about it. Just feel it.)

Companies spend millions hiring celebrities to endorse their shoes. You'll develop an emotional tie with a *hero* you admire. A recent trend is to use social media to make it seem like you're making friends with a shoe company. You know those people. They're cool. You're buddies! And their hope is that your emotional fortress will become stronger than any other shoe company can overcome. You're friends with them and they help out your heroes..

why wouldn't you buy your shoes from the friends of your friends (who are also *your* friends...according to Facebook)?

The same thing happens with elections. I always laugh when people talk about money influencing an election. If we had voters who were making rational decisions based on principles, how could money affect an election? But then again, if we were living on principle, no voting would be necessary. No amount of voting changes a principle. No amount of money changes a principle.

But if elections are held on the basis of opinions—and voting done on the basis of sentimentality and emotions—you can spend a boatload of money on advertisement to twist people's emotions (and their vote) in a particular direction. Politicians—through advertising, fear-mongering, and emotional talking points—prey on the emotions of voters.

The charade of debates fits right in with the emotional manipulation scheme. Seldom does a candidate talk about anything of any substance or reason, instead relying on ridiculous statements like, "We can be great again!" to draw applause and make them seem *electable* or *experienced.* Nobody stops to ask, "Were we great?" or "What does "great" mean?" Debates have become emotional pony shows. The goal is not to talk about real issues, but to get the voting base emotionally charged (or not make a mistake that the mainstream media will blast you for).

Elections are your slave master's way of giving you a choice (making you feel free) to become emotionally attached, while never giving you a choice in the end at all. The *lesser of two evils* is still evil. Regardless of who wins, the same system of violence and monopolization is in place.

Ever notice that each election is "THE MOST IMPORTANT ELECTION OF YOUR LIFETIME!!!!" ? The longer we are convinced that elections are real or important, the longer we fail to address any fundamental problems or principles. Illusory cheese. Elections *have been a scam for our entire lives* and beyond. We get emotionally involved in thinking that *our voice is heard.* It's difficult to take a step back and realize our voice isn't heard; the top interests always profit, few end up maintaining, and most end up worse than before (even if it doesn't seem that way, due to the temporary illusion of central banking). Elections prey on sentimental investment.

Illusory cheese and sentimental investment are important fundamentals to understand in our slavery. It's not enough to merely make another decision or convince somebody of a rational point. Unless the emotional fortress is defeated, you are anchored in place. Slave masters have discovered these powers. They have discovered how to manipulate you so you develop a positive emotional bond to working for their benefit. Look at how many people are enthusiastic about the idea of raising taxes. Almost universally, people are upset with the government. Yet half of them are convinced that giving more money to the same government (they are unhappy with) will solve anything. Since the government has been in debt for *our entire lives,* there's not any evidence that more money has ever solved anything!

A more complicated example of negative emotional investment and the emotional fortress is government itself; the government of the United States of America in particular. I am most familiar with my own government but these principles have applied to governments across time and space.

Any government is very interested in retaining (and increasing) it's power. To that end, government has created a vast web of obfuscation, confusion, and manipulation to make sure that you remain exactly where you are, if not a little worse off. People buy into this wholesale because of the negative emotional investment spun positively to government (in the form of propaganda) that we are bombarded with daily. We are also kept very busy with loads of illusory cheese.

There's all kinds of patriotism to various degrees which gets people emotionally attached to the ideas of their government, especially relative to other governments. International sports tournaments, like the Olympic Games, are powerful tools that all governments enjoy. All the people of your country, welled up with pride in their own country and, by virtue of proximity, government. There's always obligatory photos of top statesmen attending the sporting events. Nationalism encourages people to build an emotional fortress inside of themselves around the idea of the country.

Vague campaign promises are illusory cheese. *Change* is a recent political slogan that has been thrown around. Change for what? Change to what? It can turn into anything you like, in your own mind. The abstract concept fulfills several obligations. It is tailorable in each mind. It is unfulfillable in a literal sense, but rhetorically sound. Most of all, it gets our emotions going. Especially when we're upset; we all want change!

There are plenty of obvious examples that might show our own government to be corrupt. The blatant disregard for the Constitution, abuses of money, or abuses of power. Most people are able to understand...and then get on with their lives. They might get upset for a moment, or vow revenge at the next election cycle, but then it's business as usual. This baffled me until I understood sentimental investment and the emotional fortress. They might comprehend a single rational fact but the single fact is not enough to get over the massive emotional fortresses positively built around government.

It's not a matter of convincing people as to the corruption in government. They can watch/hear this and understand. What rational information cannot overcome is a host of underlying (positive) emotions attached to the government that this information is not able to climb over. It's one thing for a person to understand the literal facts of corruption. They're generally not able to *compute the implications* of what it means when the authority breaks it's own rules. Why can't they compute the implications? A huge emotional fortress of positive feelings for the government. There can't be any bad implications because ultimately the government "represents us" or is "looking out for the greater good" or (possibly worst of all) "we are the government". We want to be properly "represented", "defended", "looked out for", and nobly led. We like these ideas. They feel good. Events in reality that contradict these emotional feel-good points can be rationalized away as aberrations. Meaningless exceptions. So long as we can be manipulated to *feel* the benevolence of our overlords, they will seem benevolent to us.

Since there is no national database of police involved shootings (not exactly the kind of numbers that would benefit the government to keep statistics on), a man named Jim Fisher has compiled as much information as he can find on his True Crime blog, and come to the conclusion that 607 people were killed by police in the United States in 2011. According to the 2011 report by the National Counter Terrorism Center, *seventeen* United States citizens were killed in 2011 as a result of terrorists. As a United States citizen, you are *35 times more likely* to be killed by a police officer than a terrorist! Regardless of what the numbers show—compared with lightning strikes, car crashes, or heart attacks—we're being told that we're being "defended" from terrorism—and it feels good—so it must be true.

A common rationalization of the above point will be that the police are dealing with criminals, so of course they had to shoot them. However, you can watch videos on the internet of the executions of Oscar Grant or John T. Williams and see clear instances of murder. With a little research, you can discover dozens of stories of police violence against citizens, swept under the rug. If they change the law to make reading this book (a non-violent act) a criminal offense, and shoot you as a result, is it justified? Our automatic assumption is that police only deal with criminals. We automatically assume that when the police use violence on citizens that it is justified. We have been conditioned to accept a monopoly on violence. At what point does the initiation of violence become unacceptable? Intellectually, non-violence wins every time. Emotionally, violence is acceptable if it is against people we disagree with.

Emotional fortresses defend ideas that we are sentimentally attached to. The more emotionally attached, the bigger the fortress, the harder it is to entertain thoughts or feelings of a contrary nature. Emotional manipulation, through illusory cheese or sentimental investment, ends up ensnaring masses of people. Especially considering the duration of the bombardment (our entire lives) and when it begins (when we are very impressionable; in school).

Once an emotional attachment is screwed into place, it can be almost impossible for a mind to escape.

THE FALSE DICHOTOMY

If you wanted to guarantee somebody comes to a particular conclusion, a great way to do so is to present them with the choice you want them to make against an absurd alternative. The only key is to present them in a way whereby they seem to be the only choices. What would you like for dinner, a burrito or a rock?

If you'd like a person to avoid a particular conclusion altogether, present two alternative conclusions (as if they are the only two conclusions possible). If you wanted to avoid, at all costs, having pizza for dinner, you might ask if somebody would prefer to go eat Mexican or Thai food? The two choices gives them a choice. Since you didn't offer them an option that includes pizza, or the option of anything, you have likely corralled their mind into one of two options that are *your* preference.

This technique is brilliant for allowing the person who is presented with the options to feel as if they have freedom of choice while allowing you almost total control over the situation. So long as one option is absurd, one answer is guaranteed. Or in the case where an option is being avoided—out of sight, out of mind—alternatives of your choosing are considered first. Any possible answer to the question you would wish to avoid, simply omit.

Many discussions on the inadequacies of the current system suddenly jump to, “What's your fantasy utopia?” The person asking the question is attempting to pigeonhole the other into admitting the current system is unavoidable. Perfect has never been an option, but when did *better* get taken off the table? Believing in the (fantasy) unavoidable nature of the current system is the first step of being stuck with it forever.

The trick is understanding false dichotomies against fundamentals, in some instances, there may not be an alternative. As an example, Freedom and Slavery are antithetical, burritos and pizza are not. Oftentimes false dichotomies are manufactured when it comes to labels, rather than principles.

Are you...

Right or Left?

Democrat or Republican?

Pro-Life or Pro-Choice?

"Educated" or "Uneducated"?

For peace or for war?

A jock or a nerd?

Pro-Union or Anti-Union?

A patriot or a terrorist?

Pro-Gun or Anti-Gun?

Pro-government or Pro-business?

A good guy or a bad guy?

Evolutionist or Creationist?

With us or against us?

...or do you have a brain?

THE POWER OF WORDS

One of the greatest tools of power is words. Language is a power of its own. Words have power. Communication can shape our minds or touch our hearts. The choice and definition of words can be powerful tools in shaping the way we see the world.

"Pretty good", "alright", and "above average" could all be used to describe a particular quality about the same thing, and even though they are synonymous, they each give a different connotation. "Pretty good" can seem encouraging. "Above average" can seem like a backhanded complement. "Alright" sounds mediocre. These are light examples, but there are a variety of word manipulations that can skew our perspectives.

The way to get around language manipulation is to begin questioning it. If you start to think about the language, you'll see how it falls apart.

Political correctness is a lesson in distortion and manipulation. "Hate crimes" are somehow more hateful than other crimes? Is there such a thing as "war crimes" when half of all war actions (by the aggressor) are criminal? English Language Learner (ELL) is a term now used to describe people who were formerly English as a Second Language (ESL).

Reality being what it is; all crimes are hateful, initiating war is automatically a crime, and some people are learning a second language. Through language manipulation, groups can push particular agendas. Language manipulation facilitates mental and emotional manipulation.

We've undergone a lifetime of positive psychological bombardment about the government. Though you might hear negative things about a particular party, or portion of government, you are subjected to non-stop positive reinforcement *about* the government.

The government uses words to control your mind, screw your emotions into place, and ensure your loyalty until death. Let's start with nationalism. The government has a vested interest in making you feel nationalistic. God Bless America. God Bless the USA. Land of the Free. Home of the Brave. The greatest country in the world. The seat of western civilization. The shining city on the hill. Bringing democracy to the world. And on and on and on.

Nationalism assumes an inherent superiority, otherwise there would be no reason to be nationalistic. Nationalism is designed to make you forget internal problems; to unite against a common enemy. Nationalism, by default, is the enemy of humanity, since humans, by default, are not better than one another. The United States isn't any more moral than any other country in the world. Americans aren't any more deserving of the Earth, or to the use of it, than anyone else. Americans don't have the benefit of any natural laws the rest of the world is deprived of. That's why they are *natural laws,* they are universal! If all people are born equal, as even people in the United States assume, then that also means people born on the other side of the planet are born equal. We have our humanity in common, and then we divide against ourselves into arbitrary nation-states through nationalism.

Is one man born on a side of an arbitrary line different than the other? Legally, our government would say so. But in every other way, the two could be exactly the same. Because of government, being born on one side of a line can mean that you starve in a ghetto. Born on the other side of the line, you can waste your whole life on a couch in suburbia. One side of the line and you end up playing football for your whole life. The other side of the line, soccer.

As you already know, history is written by the victors. Being recent victors, we've colored our own history. For every one who has had their freedoms protected by the United States, the United States has certainly trampled on the freedoms of another. Is that how God has blessed the United States? By allowing a system of unsustainable, gluttonous lifestyles at the expense of underdeveloped peoples around the world? Nationalism is a false pride designed to rationalize abuses of the "others", while maintaining loyalty and obedience to "your own".

We're encouraged to be *patriotic.* Love your country. Sacrifice for your country. Duty to your country. Okay then, what is the country? Is it a land mass? Is it a race of people? An ethnicity? Is it arbitrary lines on a map? Is it an ideal? Or does *country* just mean *federal government?* If I am honest, I don't really know what our country is.

If we asked 100 citizens of the United States, "What is the United States?" how many different answers do you think we would get? Forget all the different answers, the fact that we don't have a common understanding of a single answer is the problem itself. People are being killed around the globe in the name of the United States. Are they being killed for an idea? Are they being killed for a land mass? Is it a document? A particular people? Some sort of arbitrary legal jurisdiction?

Displaying a flag, or as many flags as possible, is a display of how much you love your country, even if we aren't quite sure what the country is. Symbols of the nation are important for stirring up emotional ideas. The literal act of flying a flag doesn't make you any freer or braver, but it can instill within you an emotional sense that you are, or that you are surrounded by people who are.

We are bombarded with ideas such as nationalism or patriotism for something (the USA) abstract. At best, it's a legal jurisdiction? Seems an undue pride for a legal jurisdiction but if we can convince people to have an undue amount of pride at the expense of reason, you can do what you like in the name of the legal jurisdiction. If my legal jurisdiction is automatically superior to other legal jurisdictions, I can rationalize away any wrongdoings. I don't see people running around screaming about how much better King County is than all the other counties in Washington State. Waving King County flags. Singing King County songs. Attacking people in other counties in the name of King County defense....I'm getting ahead of myself.

The use of language is a creative way to twist your mind (and ultimately, your actions). We want to feel good. We want to feel right. We want to feel that we are on the good side of good vs. evil. Through language manipulation, it is accomplished by preying on our proclivity to apathy and comfort.

We were (allegedly) attacked by terrorists on September 11th. This was used as the basis for the war in Afghanistan, which continues to this day, 11 years later. The War on Iraq/Afghanistan/Terror/anyone is in the name of "defense". We're "defending" ourselves from the terrorists. We're not defending on our own soil, we're spending billions *defending* on sand thousands of miles away. Terrorism is touted as a humongous threat, but did you know that in the year 2011 you're more likely to be struck by lightning than killed by a terrorist?

We're thousands of miles away, *defending* ourselves. If i drove across the country and killed somebody in the name of self-defense, would a jury convict me of murder? Or acquit me in self-defense? If you can be led to believe the word "defense" mean "attack", any attack anywhere can be done in the name of (morally correct) defense. Not because of any actual change in action; the action is what it is. The words come to define the action in your mind.

Altering the meaning of a single word pacifies even your subconscious. As proof, look at how many Americans loudly advocate attacks in the name of defense.

The war against Iraq was called a "preemptive strike". This is fancy slang for "attack". It was not a defensive move. It is an attack, but attacking is unpopular. Good guys don't commit murder (in theory). That's why it needs to be called a preemptive strike. *Preemptive Strike* makes it sound as if an attack was assured but he virulent anti-war protests at the time attest to how threatened the public felt.

Whether we really would or wouldn't have been attacked means nothing. Nobody knows. We launched the attack (in the name of defense) and the rest is history. But by calling it a *preemptive strike* we add a psychological connotation that the attack is justified. It has enough of a psychological twist that it is easily rationalized without deliberately thinking about it.

It is acceptable to murder people around the globe because of the psychological manipulation! Can you go down the street and kill your neighbor because you were sure they were going to attack you? Individuals carrying out preemptive strikes would never hold up with a jury; not now, 10 years ago, or ever. The logic behind a *preemptive strike* is as follows: I can do whatever I want; ethics, morals, laws, and everyone else on the planet be damned. When murder is justifiable, anything goes. And murder becomes justifiable in the minds of people across the land when language is manipulated.

Manipulated language causes us to think and feel differently about what we are hearing. It doesn't seem like an "attack" if we call it a "preemptive strike", which is synonymous with retaliation, which seems to suggest that we'd been attacked first, which suggests that it's justifiably defensive.

Our military has bases in dozens of countries around the world, and we perform deadly missions in a variety of other countries...where does the money come from? It's *defense* spending. God forbid it should ever be called what it is; *attack* spending. *Occupation* spending. Would people tolerate being taxed for occupations? We would tolerate Iraq having military bases in the United States in the name of Iraqi defense? But *defense* is moral. Defense is justified. So long as we call murder "defense", (and assume, thanks to nationalism, that we are the only people on the planet worth defending) it is easily rationalized away. Linguistic manipulation is palatable to an ignorant, brainwashed population.

It is presented as obvious that everything our military does is very upright, since it's all in the name of defense. However, should your brain get past defense, you'll arrive at the mental hurdle of "service". These brave men and women are doing us a *service.* They're *serving* in the military. It only takes a cursory look at the definition of the word *service* to see the difficulty in arriving at this conclusion. In theory, the military *should* be performing a service (and in theory, the military should only be voluntary and take literally defensive actions; on our soil...but theories are such a long distance from reality). Once we get past all the manipulated language, military "service" hardly seems like much of a service.

Who is being helped by the military? Once we establish that there isn't much *defense* going on, I guess you'd have to belong to an oil company, private security company, or *defense* contractor to have a service done for you by the military. Those people are swimming in vaults of money like Scrooge McDuck. Maybe it's fair to say that the military is doing a *service* to companies that make weapons and countries/companies who make a profit by violently exploiting people around the globe. Is the average citizen *served* by this behavior?

The word *service* has a noble ring to it and so no matter how poorly the results might turn up, that our young men and women are engaged in such a noble-sounding task is all the pep talk our brains might need. It's *service.* Since service is noble, and we call it *service;* whatever it is they are doing is clearly noble.

Government will make it easy for you to believe in this fantasy "service". Countless television recruiting advertisements. A thousand reverent gestures. Salute the flag. Moments of silence. Sing the National Anthem before events. Remember those who *gave* their lives. Memorial Day. Veterans Day. Flag day. Independence Day. You've been *served!* Once your emotions are firmly nailed into place, your subservience is guaranteed.

Maybe they're not serving us. Maybe they're serving democracy to the rest of the world? First off, we're not a democracy. Second, you should be thanking God that we're not a democracy. Third, we shouldn't wish democracy on anyone. There's plenty written on this so I don't need to get too far into it but here's the short: In a democracy, the 51% can boss around the 49%. The will of the majority is *right.* "Everyone gets their voice heard", right before they get it stamped out if they're in the minority. Having one more person has never made a cause just. One additional person has never turned the wrong into right. It is just one more person who believes a particular way.

Democracy makes inequalities worse, since the majority always rule at the expense of the minority. Democracy is an intellectual sham that the non-thinking person buys into emotionally; and further, wishes on the rest of the world; and even further, imagines that the military/government is doing him a personal favor, a *service,* by forcing (our idea of) democracy on the rest of the world. The United States idea of "democracy" is countries who are friendly to the United States. We happily kill people in other countries when our interests get in the way of democracy, like Guatemala in 1954.

By manipulating language, we can say, “everyone gets a say” or “everyone has their voice heard” and then we can associate these kinds of ideas with justifiably right concepts such as “treating others as you want to be treated”. Everyone having their voice heard makes it (allegedly) equal.

Bullying is not acceptable on the playground, yet democracy *institutionalizes* it on a larger scale. Democracy rationalizes bullying and mob rule.

Nationalism, patriotism, defense, service, and democracy. Even looking at the words together—due to the conditioning I have experienced—all have a positive feel. Add in all the holidays in which we deify presidents or government events, the “noble service” of the “public servants” all around us, all the military recruitment commercials on television, “Army Strong!”, “The Few. The Proud.”, learning about the government in a government school, hearing the historical perspective from the side of the victors (the government), and a thousand other ways in which we are exposed to the positive (or positive word-spun manipulation) propaganda *about* the government.

Political parties participate. Republicans and democrats use abstract terms to define themselves; “conservative” and “progressive”. There's nothing conservative about policing the world or waging a war against people using a plant in their house. There's nothing progressive about social programs and monetary policy that helped ruin the Roman empire. Yet these parties espouse clever language to trick the minds of the members. These words are tossed around as ideals or principles, but are they? Is “conservative” a principle? Is “liberal” an ideal? A few moments of thought reduces the illusion to smoke, but if you can be kept in an angry emotional fervor against your opponent, you may not think about it clearly for a few moments. So you must always be riled up about "conserving" traditions or "progressing" into better territory.

The government has a masterful command of language, and as a result, they have a masterful command over the way people think. Would you be satisfied with a government who circles the globe, murdering people in your name? Of course not. Would you be satisfied with a government who is *serving* and *defending* you, while *spreading democracy?* Sounds noble enough. Notice how we don't even have to talk about the results. Regardless of whatever they're actually doing (it is what it is), your feeling is going to be very attached to what we (or they) *call* it. Thus, the power of words.

It's not just government who has a command of language. Companies have become very good at playing the game as well. Look at the food next time you go shopping. You've typically got two produce options when you're in the store. You can buy a "banana" or you can buy an "organic banana". Organic, signifying a more natural process to the making of the banana (only marginally true since the FDA is a scam), is more expensive and seen as a more luxury, niche food item.

If we think about it for a few moments, it becomes obvious how backwards our thinking is. For thousands of years, people just grew food. Bananas were bananas were bananas. Only in recent times, as chemicals have worked their way into the food growing process has a "bioengineered banana" become synonymous with "banana". In fact, it has replaced it altogether. There is no real distinction for a banana grown with (who knows what) chemicals or genetic manipulation involved in the process. "Banana" means "any banana (except those bananas that grow without/with less chemicals/manipulation)".

Since the switch was eased into existence, now we've come up with a term to quantify what happens when we cease using the newfangled chemicals (poisons) and genetic mutation. Now we refer to food with less chemicals as "organic". Food, for thousands of years, nearly all of human history, has been very close to what we we now call "organic" food. A "banana" in the present doesn't mean the same thing as "banana" a few hundred years ago.

No big deal, right? Food is a broad term. It doesn't seem like a very big deal but it's one more piece in the brainwashing puzzle. If you think of chemically altered food as being normal, you're more likely to eat it. If you view "organic" food as being a luxury item, or niche, you're less likely to buy it.

Subconsciously, the populace is susceptible to being pressed into the preferred outcomes of the elite. Language and (the lack of) transparency are vital to the system of control. If you can be led to believe in a particular view emotionally, your actions will follow in support of that view.

Language manipulation allows us to assume good intentions at all times. Results are meaningless; everyone has good intentions these days. Citizens realize they are being shafted by politicians on a daily basis, yet the go along with it because they are able to rationalize results away in the name of good intentions (or they feel that being shafted is "just the way it is", meaning that it's certain—thanks to their inaction—to be the way it always is). We're being *represented.* We're being *served.* They consider the *public good. The general welfare.* If we observe and analyze results, if we question the definitions of the language, the reality of good intentions vanishes.

We are taught (by the government and their friends in the mainstream media) that our government always has our best interest in mind. Results, dating back to the beginning of recorded history, are almost all stacked in contrary to this presumption, yet we are drilled over and over to have faith in the goodwill of our superiors. This has the effect of creating a never ending political dialogue in this country, much to the benefit of those in control. A thousand times a day, we hear, “It just doesn't make any sense that Joe Politician would do...” and it doesn't ever matter what it is that he/she is doing. Anything. “Why would they ever let our currency get devalued?” Almost all political action seems nonsensical if we assume good intentions and if we assume good intentions we allow a wide berth for terrible results.

Next time you're confused, attempt to analyze the situation from the perspective of negative intentions. Be prepared to be shocked at how many pieces of the puzzle fall into place. In a country where you assume good intentions, the passage of a 2,000 page piece of legislation —sponsored (sometimes written) by large corporate interests, which is so large and sudden that nobody has the chance to read it—seems baffling. Would a just government pass a law without reading it? Wouldn't any sensible government read the law before voting on it? What the heck is going on? But if you assume you are in an environment of nefarious intentions, collusion, obfuscation, and hidden agendas, all of a sudden the nonsense makes much more sense...

Words are powerful. Definitions can be tweaked to change the meaning, emotionally. Such is the case with “democracy”. I used to think democracy was a just and brilliant system. Why shouldn't everyone “have a say”? I learned the reality of democracy and discovered it to be just as evil as many other forms of evil government. With a twisted meaning, it's not so easy to spot the flaws. “Governed by the people.” “Everyone has a say.”

"Everyone's voice is heard." "Everyone is represented." Democracy *feels* good, even if almost half of the people suffer.

In other cases, language can be completely changed. "Defense" now means "attack". Anything can mean anything. You have to untangle the linguistic mystery in order to begin to articulate your complaint. It's another layer of the slave master's defense. Manipulative language, on the surface, gives validity to nonsense. In a world of nonsense, people are encouraged to make emotional(ly manipulated) decisions.

If your mind is unable to untangle the language, it's much harder for you to become upset. The easier it is for your mind to rationalize something away, all the more likely that you'll do so. If you have built a massive emotional fortress before you are able to critically think for yourself, it's all the more likely that you'll never learn to think for yourself.

Words have immense power. How you listen will shape your perception. How you speak will shape the perspectives of others. Perception is 51% of reality. In fact, our perceptions become reality. Words can build the world, destroy the world, or twist the world for specific purposes.

FREEDOM, THE MORAL PRINCIPLE

Many words have their meanings twisted for nefarious purposes. Stretching the meaning of the word "defense" gives us liberty to justifiably attack another.

Nowhere does linguistic manipulation damage citizens as seriously as the damage that has been done to the word *Freedom.* Any deviation away from the real understanding of Freedom is naturally a deviation toward slavery; it's antithesis. I cannot, at the same time, be a slave and a free man. The onset of slavery is the end of Freedom.

The damage done to the word Freedom, and it's subsequent meaning, is a damage felt throughout every aspect of our lives. Freedom, in it's essence, has one meaning and one exception (because it cannot contradict itself). The meaning is this: you are free to make absolutely *any* choice. Freedom, a natural and universal right of every person on the planet, allows each of us to do as we wish. The one exception is this: you cannot make a choice which impedes on the freedoms of another. You are not free to make a choice that restricts the choice of another. You can not initiate violence on another.

Simply illustrated: You are free to grow your own food. You are not free to capture another human and force them to grow your food for you. You are free to work where you like. You are not free to force another person to work as a slave for you. You are free to say whatever you like. You are not free to stop other people from saying whatever they like. You are free to defend yourself with deadly force if you are attacked with deadly force. You are not free to initiate deadly force on another.

The moral principle should appear very clear. You are free to live in whatever manner you should choose so long as you do not impair another's ability to live in the manner they choose.

The result of defining freedom differently means we treat each other differently. Since Freedom no longer means that "you are free to do as you like so long as you do not impede on the freedom of another", the general public does not see an impairment of their freedom as being wrong. If you don't understand Freedom, you don't understand if you have it or not. The general definition of the word is based on opinions so it can have any number of meanings.

Thanks to the new definition, freedom means something like, "you are free to do exactly as I would do". One person sees their way of living as moral, therefore all people "are free" to live within those bounds. Freedom is not a principle. Freedom is an opinion. We are not expected to live under a universal code. We are expected to live under the code of whosever opinion of freedom is in fashion. We are "free" to do as they say.

Democrats believe everyone should have the freedom to be a democrat, and a democrat only. Republicans believe everyone should have the freedom to live as a republican, and a republican only. Socialists believe everyone should have the freedom to only live as a socialist. Tyrants, Kings, Monarchs, Presidents (including the President of the United States), and bodies of legislature (such as the House of Representatives and the Senate) all believe that all of their peasants should be free to live exactly as they allow them to live. Never are we governed by a moral principle, but by an opinion. Why? Because the population now (and often in the past) believes the definition of Freedom is an opinion, not a moral principle, so the concept of being governed by opinion, rather than principle, is tolerable. If you do not understand the principle of Freedom, you cannot complain if you don't have it.

Government often argues that they must restrict certain freedoms for the general maintenance of Freedom. Not only is this logic a slippery slope, it eventually devolves into complete slavery. We must give up a right to privacy in order to have the right to travel. TSA frisks people at the airports and is now moving toward highway stops and searches. We are told we must give up Freedoms (such as those listed in the Bill of Rights) in order for the government to keep us safe. Except, the Bill of Rights keeps the citizenry safe in the first place. Is a society without basic rights worth protecting?

The general public tolerates it because they all desire to be free. If Freedom means "free to do as you're told" then it works every time. Since the definition of the word freedom—no longer a principle but an opinion—is the opinion of whomever is in power, all we need to do is elect the person into office who has the idea of freedom most closely matching my own. This is not Freedom. This is the opinion of freedom (slavery) dressed in Freedom's clothes.

Through this ruse, almost every citizen in the nation, perhaps the entire world, is a hypocrite. Each imagines that every other person on the earth should live exactly as they imagine themselves free to live. Each thinks that the laws of the land should be tailored so that freedom is guaranteed exactly as they imagine freedom being guaranteed to protect their own interests. You should live as I live. Everyone else should live as citizens of the United States lives. And so on.

A lack of Freedom underlines the evil nature of monopolistic government; one is the master and one the slave. There is no neutral in government. In any government not governed by moral principle, you either make the rules or you have the rules made on you.

In the "Land of the Free", not only is nobody free, but few understand what Freedom even means.

SOLVING SURPLUS THROUGH ADDITION

Ghandi is quoted as saying, "an eye for an eye makes the whole world blind".

In times past, when the mafia had a much stronger influence, the mob had clear methods of problem solving. Each time a group is violated, they take (what they perceive as) equal retribution. No doubt, this left the other side feeling unjustly violated, so they must take retribution. Mafia families were killing each other indefinitely in the name of the original crime, much like the Hatfields and McCoys. This method of problem solving is *solving surplus through addition.*

Murder is an extreme example. Thanks to the finality of death, there's no real way to undo the deed. However, we experience a thousand lesser cases on a daily basis where the scales are tipped and we—rather than remove the imbalance—merely shuffle who the imbalance falls on. Law is a great example: upon perceiving injustice, the injustice is rarely removed. Usually, a counterbalancing injustice is added on the other end of the scale. We never end up with any principled laws or governance; every law is merely an attempt at swinging the pendulum of justice in favor of one person over another, depending in who is in charge or which angry demographic must be pacified.

Starting at the empty scale of Freedom, a principle applying universally to all, a weight (a law) is placed on one end to favor one group of people. Let's use the laws providing taxation rates (ignoring that taxation is theft) clearly in favor of one particular group. Out of this codified inequality arises a need to place a weight on the other end to compensate the recently disenfranchised.

We'll make another law giving some benefit to some group that was taken advantage of in the first law. The scale is still unbalanced so we make another law to give some other group another benefit. Inequality after inequality codified into law. Infinite—and meaningless—adjusting of tax percentages. The injustice will go on forever, since the real issues are never addressed; the evils of taxation, the monopoly on land, the central manipulation of the currency, etc. Citizens become divided against each other (rich against poor) instead of working together against a common enemy (taxation, theft, monopolization, violence).

Since the law was crooked to begin with, somehow we can make more laws to further dispel injustice? Unjust legislation is the *cause* of the problem in the first place! The common mode of operation is *exactly the opposite* of how we ought to think. Rather than add to injustice in another way, injustice should be removed.

Unfortunately, solving surplus with addition is a principle rampant in modern society. Men have been abusive to women. Rather than advocate for the removal of dysfunction, we create an equally dysfunctional group; feminists. Entire societies of people have been impoverished through unjust legislation, so we create more legislation with the wording and sentiment of charity, which keeps them impoverished for eternity. The State creates a legal fiction based on a religious sacrament, marriage, which discriminates against particular people. Rather than remove the state's influence in marriage, the only conceivable option is for the state to wholly run all marriage. Did government cause a problem? The common train of thought is that government can fix it. Should fix it. Will fix it. Observing the ever-growing litany of social problems, the government is amassing quite a track record...of failure.

Solving surplus through addition works perfectly with language manipulation. It plays off of our natural desire for “an eye for an eye” and the emotional fortresses we have built up around our opinions of freedom. Injustice, solved with injustice, perpetuating injustice. This selfish, unprincipled way of thinking, or of building a society, is the very definition of incompetence, insanity, or both.

COMPROMISE

> "All compromise is based on give and take, but there can be no give and take on fundamentals. Any compromise on mere fundamentals is a surrender. For it is all give and no take." -Ghandi

There's nothing wrong with working together or mutual understanding, but neither of those has anything to do with compromise. Compromise is a moving away from the original position. Compromise is a lessening. Compromise is storing your sand in a cracked hourglass; as time passes, you inevitably have less. Any compromise away from Freedom results in less Freedom.

Compromise is not universal. Death, gravity, and imperfection all *are.* Government compromises with citizens as little as it must to retain power. Law doesn't compromise; guilty or not-guilty.

Compromise is what evil people use to convince you to let go—to consent of being swindled—of anything worth holding onto.

PERCEPTIONS

I was visiting friends in San Diego a few summers back. For whatever reason, we decided to go swimming in the Pacific Ocean around 1am. Around midnight, a few friends showed up and a cool breeze was blowing in as we started changing into our board shorts and swim suits.

One girl, Kristina, brought her boyfriend Collin along for the swim, but I noticed he wasn't changing into anything—just standing there with his arms crossed. I asked him if he brought some board shorts; he had. I asked him if he was going to change into them; he wasn't. "You guys will probably only swim for two seconds anyway. I'm not going to get changed for that; it's cold out."

The rest of us changed anyway, as Collin teased Kristina about her upcoming non-swim. As we walked the few blocks to the water, Collin got in a few more points about how cold it was, how cold the water was, and how miserable swimming in the freezing ocean would be.

We got to the water. The breeze was much crisper as we got down to nothing but trunks. A couple toes went in. A couple shrieks rang out. A couple ankles went in. More shrieks. But submerged ankles led to submerged knees, which soon led to submerged legs. Within a few minutes, five of us were jumping on the ocean floor, neck deep, as Collin stood on the beach forty feet away.

The moon was bright. The breeze was fresh. Ocean Beach was dark, except for a few street lights. And we jumped and yelled and swam in the pitch black waves for about ten minutes until Kristina decided to go back to shore because "Collin was all by himself". The rest of us jumped around and swam for another twenty minutes or so, while they stood on the beach, and then we rejoined the two of them, went back to the house and turned in for the evening.

I don't remember a lot, and I don't remember a lot about that trip, but that night has stayed with me as the night I understood the effects of perception. The temperature of the ocean was what it was. The breeze was as cool as it was. It was late, dark, and possibly foolish. But we had two distinct experiences that night due to perceptions.

Most of us had a somewhat positive outlook. We weren't certain about the experience but we were willing to give it a shot. Swimming in the ocean at night seemed like it could be fun; so we gave it a go. Turned out, it was extremely fun. It stands out in my mind as a unique landmark amongst good experiences.

On the other hand, Collin had the same opportunity—he even brought the board shorts—but he didn't even take it. I'd bet money that he has long forgotten about that night. All he did was go meet up with some friends, stand on the cold beach for half an hour, and go home. Entirely forgettable, if not miserable.

The differences in our experiences were the result in the differences in our actions, which were the result of the differences of our perceptions. Our experiences that night were shaped *first* by how we thought the night would go. It turned out to be a self-fulfilling prophecy either way (positive or negative).

In how many other ways do our perceptions shape our realities? How different is our perception from reality?

It should come as no surprise that the first step to maintaining the system (by those in control) is to control the perception of the system. Howard Zinn has famously demonstrated how the traditional narrative of history has been skewed to color (our perception of) the past. The control of reality relies on the control of perception; news, media, marketing, public relations—manipulations.

DIVISION AND CONQUEST

Doesn't it seem wild to imagine that a few people can control millions? How is this ever possible? For a concrete example, we can look to plantations of the old south; the ones that had dozens of slaves and a single owner. The hierarchy was designed for a single slave owner to maintain control over multiple lives. On the surface, it seems impossible. The slaves could easily, physically overcome the master but there were many reasons why slaves remained as slaves (outside of technical deficiency, though that plays a small part).

The law was on the side of the owner. The slaves were psychologically beaten into submission; convinced of their own inferiority. The slaves were kept busy and stupid. Information was controlled. Logic was twisted.

The plantations of the old south teach us a lot about our current conditions. One of the most devastating techniques is *conquest through division.*

It should be obvious that a handful of people would not be able to control a hundred million people if the masses were united under a common ideal. Overlords need the masses to work for them. They have to eat. They don't want to grow their own food. Rulers have to build their own houses. They don't want to do these things, obviously, otherwise they'd already be doing them. They want you and I to do it. They want us to fight each other for the privilege of building their houses and growing their food. Then they want us to fight each other so they can remain in power. It should be obvious that almost none of the people in power actually believe in Freedom. If they did, they'd set you free. If people in power believed in Freedom, they wouldn't uphold a system of oppressive monopolies.

So how do a handful of people control billions? The model was executed in the old south. First, they create a group below themselves; overseers. By elevating a few slaves above their former position, you secure their loyalty and pit them against former peers. In the old south, this was accomplished with mostly poor white folks. It was a cementing of the race rift we are still experiencing today.

There's the issue of the remaining population, but they're controlled easily if you can keep them divided amongst each other. The ones who blindly accept authority are the easiest. Some will put their heads down and work. Some will preach tolerance. Some can be scared into submission. And you're left with a few who run or fight for Freedom. If an example can be made of them, the rest can likely be kept in line. Just like on the plantation. Just like republicans and democrats. Bickering indefinitely, resolving nothing.

Slaves fought amongst each other over their condition. Poor white folks were set up just above them to keep them in line. Apathetic free folks (mostly) did nothing. And so the power structure of a few slave masters (backed by the law and violence, of course) ran for decades.

The oligarchs control the overseers with land, law, money, and power. The remaining population, in large part, cancels itself out. Half of the population fights the other half. The overseers are capable of using enough violence to subjugate any overspill; any who might try to use violence against the monopoly on violence; the overseers or their masters.

The overseers and slave holders of the old South could never have stopped a full slave rebellion. They were able to maintain control of the slaves for so long, not through direct force on the slaves, but by a system of ignorance, apathy, violence, and dividing half of the population against itself.

A handful of people cannot control hundreds, or even millions. A handful of people who can convince half of an ignorant, apathetic population to fight/enslave the other half works masterfully to control millions. That's how the system works now. Divide and conquer. Republicans and democrats are a clear cut example of this strategy. When republicans win, who wins? The state and their business/banking friends. When democrats win, who wins? The state and their elite friends. So long as republicans and democrats fight each other, the elite coalition of bankers, politicians, and big business interests will keep on winning.

There's simply not any evidence to the contrary. Look at the size and powers of government over our lifetime. Look at the two party system. The two go hand in hand. For the last hundred years, the citizenry has been fighting itself for the benefit of the state and big business.

Every "social program" is evidence to this point. Even the strongest proponents of various social programs will admit that the program itself isn't ideal, but it's some sort of necessary stop-gap measure. The right question is, what motivated the measure in the first place? If Social Security, Medicare, Medicaid, Welfare, Unemployment, Affirmative Action, etc, aren't ideal programs, why were they begun?

Only a fool would argue that any of these programs have solved a problem. They were never intended to. If they had been engineered to solve a problem, their own termination would have been engineered also; when the problem was solved. Since a resolution wasn't a motive, they must have had an ulterior motive. The ulterior motive is to either get votes from a demographic (furthering the illusion of consent and power) or to pacify a demographic (as concessions from the civil rights movement have pacified minorities).

As a double bonus, these stop-gap measures become powerful tools for fracturing the populace against itself;

buffering those in power. That people are "helped" by social programs is irrelevant, since the system itself has created the situation in which they were abused in the first place—meaning the actual solution is a removal of the problem. Government creates a crooked environment in which millions are crushed under the weight of poverty, government tosses a bone to those crushed, the populace bickers amongst each other over the pseudo-solution. The various layers of government, bureaucracy, laws, and media further obscure, confuse, and distract whole segments of the population. Evil has diversified itself brilliantly.

Textbook Control 101: Cause a problem. Propose a pseudo-solution (since any real solution would involve not causing the problem to begin with). Commence never-ending argument over pseudo-solution. Problem never solved. Control maintained. Original issue (original causation of problem) never addressed. Power secure.

Control works through dividing ordinary people against each other and preying on our natural inclination to sit by and watch it happen; laziness. If you do not provide any resistance, you (even inadvertently) go along with whatever is happening. Momentum continues by default. Each person fighting his neighbor cancels the other out. There's very few people remaining to speak out or fight against the powers that be; people are so busy standing idly by or fighting each other.

Each layer in the diversification of evil increases the ability to get the population fighting each other. The more the population is divided, the more easily they are conquered. The two party system works brilliantly to split people against each other. Each issue on which they are pseudo-divided is one more issue for people to get locked into and endlessly bicker about. Nationalism comes into play at the end by taking people's minds off of internal problems and focusing energies together against a foreign enemy.

Control is simple when we are busy trying to control each other. In the end, we'll ruin ourselves if we don't realize the effects of our infighting over unprincipled opinions. People can only be united under principle and Natural Law.

Every time we put chains on another, every time we fight our neighbor—or stand idly by while they are chained—we reinforce an atmosphere in which we are destined to be chained ourselves.

Don't just take my word for it..

> Frederick Douglass put it eloquently, "No man can put a chain about the ankle of his fellow man without at last finding the other end fastened about his own neck."
>
> Martin Luther King Jr., "Injustice anywhere is a threat to justice everywhere."
>
> Martin Niemöller:
>
> First they came for the communists,
> and I didn't speak out because I wasn't a communist.
>
> Then they came for the trade unionists,
> and I didn't speak out because I wasn't a trade unionist.
>
> Then they came for the Jews,
> and I didn't speak out because I wasn't a Jew.
>
> Then they came for me
> and there was no one left to speak out for me.

INHERENT EVIL

A government that does not allow Freedom only perpetuates injustice.[1] As such, law is used as a vehicle for perpetuating one particular interest over another. An atmosphere is created in which a person then has two choices:

1- Influence the law to align with your ideals: other people are forced live as you wish.

2- Have the ideals of others forced upon you: you are forced to live as others wish.

And slavery becomes institutionalized. Each person is forced with the choice of forcing their ideals onto others, or having other's ideals forced onto them.

Even unconsciously, we realize this. At least half of all political energy is created by fear; the fear that some evil person will force their ideals onto you. How many democrats are only deathly afraid of republicans? And vice versa?

And so governance, law itself, becomes a means by which slavery is institutionalized. Each law becomes another division of masters and slaves; who will make the rules and who will be forced into them. Who will be the master? Who will be the slave?

---

1 Frederic Bastiat explained in "The Law" how a government cannot *do* anything for Freedom, it can only *not perpetuate injustice.* A concept we have seen less and less since 1781.

IMAGINATION

One of the most difficult tasks possible is to think of something you have never thought of before. Try it. Stop for a moment and try to think of something you have never thought of before...

Our thoughts become our reality. Oftentimes, individuals do not struggle with intellectually understanding principle or fundamentals, but are unable to imagine the kind of world something different would bring about. Our imaginations are hindered by self-imposed limits and beset by negative assumptions.

The government can claim that police keep us safe—from each other and from any other influences that may want to harm us—and in a rhetorical sense, it is true. However, this can only be rhetorically true with underlying assumptions that we are all helpless and somebody would certainly come to rob or kill us. Are we all helpless? Is there any imminent threat? We automatically think that without police we would be thrust into rampant violent conflict, and be destroyed. Certain realities of police protection conveniently go unmentioned; that it is also possible for us to suffer unwarranted harm or death from police (and many have) and because of the federal government's adventurism we are all constantly under the threat of nuclear attack.

Automatic assumptions poison the minds and restrict the imagination of many. "Without government roads, we wouldn't have roads!" Nevermind that people have existed without government roads for much of existence. The argument makes the assumption that, without government roads, everyone would sit around; starving to death. The feeble-minded (a creation of institutionalized school) are unable to imagine a world where people came together and create a transportation solution on their own, nonviolently, for the benefit of all. Because they are unable to imagine it, they are unable to become emotionally interested in the idea. It may be principled, it may be possible, but if it is not conceivable it is a fantasy.

Why are we still driving cars, 100 years after automobile technology began? In part, perception. People want to commute in cars. In larger part, government regulations restrict imagination. Air/space regulations, laws influenced by oil/transportation interests, safety regulations, and roads all impact our available transportation options. If government wasn't restricting what was possible, who knows how people could be transporting now. Personal heli/hover/flying/alternative energy powered craft could be running wild. Nobody really knows what could be possible. However, when government forces you to drive with four wheels on the ground—under the threat of injury or death—then people stop dreaming about the reaches of space and technology; their minds become grounded as well. So, it's true that government roads allow us to drive around. It's also true that government interference keeps us driving around.

If there's one service that humanity needs rendered, it is inspiring the imagination; imagining of a world without institutionalized violence and institutionalized monopolies. Imagining that world is the first step toward living there. Once we can imagine a better future, we can work together to dismantle the monopolies that stand in the way of arriving there.

ASSASSINATION

In a debate, discussion, or argument, the first person to call names is the one who surrenders. The namecaller automatically concedes, due to a lack of intellectual contribution. Resorting to personal attacks, known as the logical fallacy *ad hominem,* is the sign of having exhausted all legitimate contributions to the matter at hand. It is often referred to tactically as character assassination, and it is extremely powerful.

Character assassination is a powerful tool utilized on the feebleminded to encourage them to rationalize the issue at hand. If you can be convinced to dismiss any legitimate potential in an issue based on an irrelevant—typically trivial—point, then the merits of the matter at hand will never be seriously considered.

Oftentimes, in mainstream discussion, people who question the common narrative can be dismissed with a wave of the hand as “conspiracy theorists” or “crazy” or “lunatics”. What if they were raising a legitimate question? What if the common narrative defies the facts (ex:Sept 11th)? Doesn't matter. The questioners are crazy, and we don't entertain the ideas of crazy people. Problem solved. The official narrative carries on, unharmed, and those who would question authority are sullied.

I can imagine much of the resistance to this book is going to focus on how “extreme” my views are, how “uneducated” or “radical” I am, rather than a logical discussion or critique on the merits of the ideas. It'll work out well for the establishment; many people will be dissuaded from reading a book by the stupid extremist.

SYSTEMATIC CONTROL

The chart on the following page lays out the hierarchies of monopoly in modern society. The internal controls described in the previous half of the book show how a person gets caught in the cycle at the bottom of the chart. In the second half, I'll describe a general outlay, and purpose, of some of the monopolies. Violence is certainly at the top, but schooling is perhaps the most destructive. Schooling lays the foundation for a slave society by churning out mentally crippled youths faster than any other device. A society can never remain free when government begins to shape whole generations to it's own purposes. You can also see how the banking cartel (with a currency monopoly) is able to control economies and drive wealth upward.

Hopefully the chart can show how meaningless slave-on-slave violence is (such as Democrats and Republicans fighting amongst each other). Hopefully the chart also displays how involved we are in our own enslavement. Noble policemen help funnel the money upward and keep the populace in line. If law serves the masters (does the person living paycheck-to-paycheck imagine the law is serving them?) who is everyone sworn to uphold the law serving?

A: The masters.

The monopolies are diversified, but you'll see all the responsibilities and powers of monarchs of times past. This can only mean one thing: We are all peasants, just like times past.

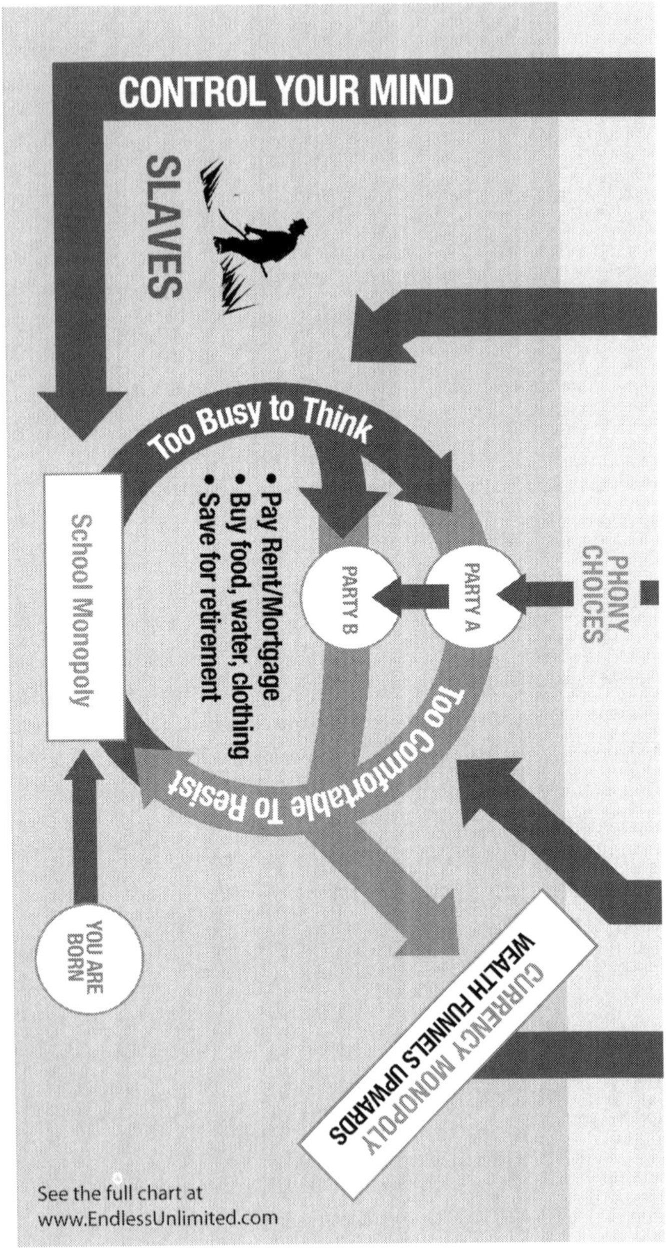

See the full chart at
www.EndlessUnlimited.com

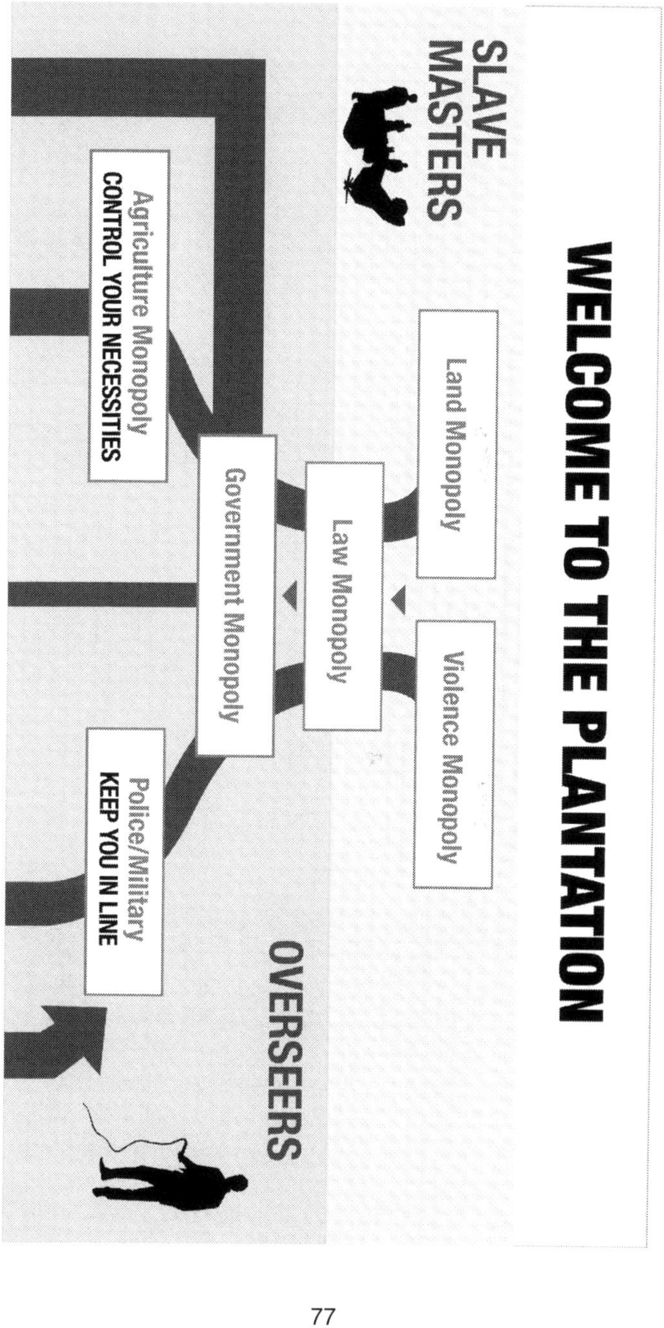
WELCOME TO THE PLANTATION
SLAVE MASTERS
Land Monopoly
Violence Monopoly
Law Monopoly
Government Monopoly
Agriculture Monopoly
CONTROL YOUR NECESSITIES
Police/Military
KEEP YOU IN LINE
OVERSEERS

SCHOOL MONOPOLY

There are fewer captivating sights than to watch a child discover the world. Watching the discovery of self-awareness seems a miracle; watching a canvas paint itself. Children are beautiful. Children are the hope for the future. No matter the situations in the present, we always dream that children will make them better. The potential of any child seems to be unlimited. They can become the future *anything*. They will do the future *anything*.

I am convinced that the greatest advantage any person can have in the world is to have a loving, supportive family. I also realize that many people aren't fortunate to begin life with this advantage. This topic is tangental, but I feel it needs to be mentioned since the argument for school always begins as an emotional plea for the unfortunate (whom I also sympathize with); at best, a community can come together to nurture the disadvantaged children. **No institution can replace a family.**

Regardless of family environment, when all children become old enough to begin developing their minds, we send them off to school. The unlimited hope for the future. The unlimited potential. The growth of a new spirit. Unlimited curiosity. Energy. Motivation. Risk-taking. The blossoming of a new personality, sent to school....sent to be crushed. Pressed into conformity. Children are the exquisite hope for the future; a hope that is extinguished on a daily basis within the institutionalized halls of school.

Once a person can read, write, speak, and count; the world is unlocked. In terms of technical skills, what more do you need? Each of us will perform technical tasks for a lifetime. Yet, without knowing the tasks, how could we pretend to know what tasks one will need to be equipped for? All the best qualities that will serve a person in life are not tangibly measured, nor acquired in the same manner as reading, writing, speaking, and counting. Honesty. Curiosity. Willingness. Motivation. A positive attitude. Creativity. Perseverance. Industriousness. Integrity. Respect. The ability *to think.* Did you learn any of these qualities from listening to lectures? Did you learn them from writing book reports or essays? Filling in multiple choice bubbles? Maybe persevering through tedium?

Many arguments in favor of schooling were more valid a hundred years ago. Schools used to be something of a gatekeeper; books, computers, access to learned minds. Today? Not so. Libraries, the Internet, and email have eliminated every technical advantage of schooling with the exception being in the company of the instructors which—if any statistics as to the failings of education are correct—is a greatly diminishing benefit. There is no longer any gatekeeper to information.

In looking at the world, in countless conversations with my peers, every conscious decision boils down to *the way* a person thinks (or that they make an effort not to). Outside of the home they grew up in, a child learns *what* or *how* to think in school. I'm very careful not to say that a child learns *to think* in school, because most children don't. With rare exception, children are drilled into a particular, generic mold. They are taught *how to think* or *what to think.* Due to a series of manipulations and tricks, we're all led to believe that people are capable of critically thinking once they leave school but there is little evidence to support the claim. If school produces legions of intelligent, creative thinkers, why is our nation such a mindless train wreck? Why does the entire population seem clueless on what is wrong with the economy? How can we have spent decades with the same two parties, each continuing horrible policies and neither solving a thing? Problems are mounting faster than they are being solved, and we are "educated"? If we study the history of public schooling in the United States (which is never studied in school, curiously enough), education—critical thinking—was never the intention.

School can be traced back to the Academy of ancient Greece, of which Plato was was once the head. Plato's Academy wasn't so much a school as we might think about it; the Academy seems to be a grove of trees where scholars and pupils met. Plato's school wasn't institutionalized anything like schooling of the present; the school was a place that scholars met to discuss and better learn the working of life. Under the olive trees dedicated to Athena, like-minds met to further their intellectual and spiritual pursuits.

Education today hasn't changed at all from education of thousands of years ago. Education is still the development of the individual. The roots of the word *education* mean "to draw out from within" or "to bring forward". Becoming educated is invaluable. Becoming educated is also intangible; at what point do you reach the goal?

What has changed over thousands of years is a masterful manipulation of language; to make "education" mean "school". The two could hardly be further apart. Education is one of the most valuable assets a person can have, or one of the most noble pursuits. Becoming educated is never ending. Education is life long. The education of a person has no limit.

School, on the other hand, is a building where you are made to conform to classes, teachers, and the abstract concept of grades, rules, and curriculum. Any unique feature you might have possessed beforehand is pressed out in the name of conformity, uniformity, repetition, and "education". School ends when you graduate. School is a place where you learn mostly theory and gain very little experience. Children are forced to visit the not-so-scenic outlook of school. They return as adults with the postcard, neatly framed at the office.

Theoretically, school at it's best could be considered a passing of time. Unfortunately, as time is finite and our greatest resource, a mere passing of time is a waste of time; time that could otherwise be valuably spent (and I don't mean money, I also mean relationships, learning, discovering, adventure, etc). At a minimum, anything valuable learned in school can be learned in the world outside—and more besides. People are naturally attracted to useful knowledge and skills that will benefit their survival and enjoyment of life. If school was a voluntary waste, it would simply be a matter of buyer beware. Since school is a forced ordeal—at least through high school—each worthless moment forced onto a child is a moment stolen. Being forced to waste your life is no better than theft or prison.

I just had a conversation with a friend's wife who is going to school to be a special education teacher. She mentioned additional programs for special education students after they graduate (from 18-21 years old). "Why would they need additional programs after graduation?" I asked. "Because when they graduate they don't have any life skills." Huh? This is coming from somebody who is training to be a teacher...so what exactly are children learning in school if they aren't learning skills that apply to living?

The same could be said for social programs. If school was churning out independent, productive people—who collectively form a productive society—why would we need such a vast network of handouts? School can't claim to be educating people in useful life skills if so many people are without useful life skills, can it? The life of every person on the receiving end of a financial aid program is evidence to the contrary of the effectiveness of the stated goals of school (and government). Additionally, look at all the social programs—including the military—which help people "go back to school". Back to school? If the first 12-16 years didn't give you what you needed, what will 2-4 more do? It is amazing to consider the centuries of possibly productive life that have been tossed into the landfill of school; forever wasted.

Since most of schooling knowledge is not applied, most of schooling knowledge is detrimental; time spent traveling in a wrong direction is time spent amounting to nothing or time spent backtracking later (if the wrong direction is ever realized). Children develop habits in school that will jeopardize their ability to think for themselves in the future; foremost among these the reliance on a class before attempting a new venture.

All the suckers in school getting business degrees before trying to start a business are the proof. Business degrees take four years and cost tens of thousands of dollars. Within the same time and money, the student could be running a successful business. Four years of real world experience and momentum of making money instead of starting from scratch, upon graduation, with no (or little) income and debt.

By dictating how and what to think, the unrealized implication also means a dictation of how not to think and what not to think about. Forcing children into a specific curricula means they are also forced away from other curricula. Hence, the unending (and completely trite) argument as to whether to teach creationism or evolution in public schools. Both of these groups realize that school is not teaching children *how to think,* but dictating to them *what to think.*

As much as I'd like to think college is a matter of buyer beware—since it's not forced on children—we have to take into account how much they have been brainwashed and peer pressured into college. They've been told for 2/3rds of their formative years—in an insulated environment of elementary/high school, as they've been pressed into conformity and drilled into submission—that college is a necessity unless they want to be a failure; only the most formidable minds can resist. I am sad to admit that I was unable to resist. Without life experience, I was unable to articulate my complaint.

The lack of comparative life experience is key to school maintaining the illusion of worth. Almost universally, people will admit they learned "more in the first year on the job than in school/college" right before they backtrack into something like "but I couldn't have done it without school." Well...why not? We operate under the assumption that if we hadn't spent years inside of school—admittedly learning little—that we would have learned less out in the world? Except, as the logic just went, people admit to having learned vastly more out of school than in.

I suppose the argument is that school was the precursor to the learning that took place out in the world; the learning gained in school was required before the learning in the world could have taken place. More flaccid logic. Didn't we each learn *before* we ever attended school? We learned from our families and friends; how to speak, walk, eat, play, and many more basics in life from the experts around us.

From birth, you learned from somebody who knew and you learned from experience. You didn't learn to walk by taking a multiple choice test. You didn't learn to eat by writing essays about eating. You didn't learn to speak, talk, or interact with people by being lectured. Nothing we have learned in life that sets the foundations for the rest of our education was achieved in school, but our education has been interrupted—often permanently deterred—by forcibly sending children to school. Even though we began life learning from experts and experience, and will learn the rest of our lives from experts and experience, we are exiled to this separate place where we are drilled narrow theory from teacher taught teachers. Once schooling is finished, we will go out into the world to learn from experience and experts once again. One of these things does not belong. That's the point here, the very concept of school is illogical. School disrupts, hinders, and even destroys education.

It is almost impossible to learn important facets of life in school because important facets of life are learned *by living!* School creates an artificial environment where failure is without consequence, as is success. Can you learn to live without living? As much as school removes children from interacting with the real world, school removes children from the only place they can learn about life. Important lessons in life can only be learned about in a classroom to the extent that soccer can be learned about in a classroom, or going to another country can be learned about in a classroom. You learn *something*—as the argument goes—but a pittance compared with what you learn from visiting another country or kicking a ball around on a soccer field (and at a fraction of the cost). For example, you never hear a soccer player say that the most valuable things he learned about the game were learned in a classroom. How often have you received the travel advice "Skip visiting the country, reading the Lonely Planet travel guide was better."?

We each had the knowledge, tools, and motivation—from the experts at hand—before ever attending school, why couldn't our learning and development as people continue to occur outside of school? Why couldn't the circle of experts and accumulated knowledge and skills continue to grow organically with the child? I can certainly recognize the challenges of exploiting and controlling massive amounts of people through such a decentralized alternative.

The bottom line is that school is merely the first step in a lifetime of control. Schools shape the way people think, control the influences into what they think, and instill an emotional fortress around the establishment of school and authority itself by emotionally correlating school and education (with the manipulation of language). This emotional fortress ensures two benefits to school itself; an automatic defensive response to any attack on school as well as pressuring any unschooled person to become schooled. As soon as you begin to question the validity of school, people bristle at the affront on *education,* as if they were the same.

There are two ways a person learns. The most obvious is through experience. The second is from somebody who knows (listening to them, reading their work). School attempts to teach you by learning from a *teacher* or *educator* (if we call it education, it must be educating; if we call them educators, they must be educating). An obvious flaw is that the teachers are typically only equipped with the knowledge they are teaching. Most teachers are just teachers, they aren't mathematicians, scientists, musicians, lawyers, doctors, biologists, artists, craftsmen, or laborers. Most true stewards of valuable information are busy plying their trades. Teachers typically don't have a real world experience to draw from; they're just teachers. Would you rather learn art from a teacher or from an artist? Would you rather learn medicine from a teacher or a doctor? Would you rather learn business from a teacher or a CEO?

Teachers understand the theoretical basics of what they are teaching but have very little (if any) experience with any subject. We have teachers teaching kids who will graduate, become teachers, and then teach kids who will become teachers. Teachers teaching teachers is a fantastic model for ignorance (and job security). Teachers are the last people you'd want to learn anything from, since few of them have applied the knowledge in a serious way themselves. Knowledge that has been applied in life is hard to find in school, since people who are applying knowledge are difficult to find in schools. Knowledge from experts in every field is easy to find outside schools; experts are outside school, working.

One of the seminal evil achievements of school has been institutionalizing the separation of theory from experience. Learn the theory of law, never experience law (through going to court, shadowing a lawyer). Learn math, rarely apply math. Copy a scientific experiment, rarely conduct your own experiment. Write a book report, never write a book. Learn the concept of a business plan, never start a business. Learn about government, never participate in governance. Is it any surprise many people exit school with little understanding of the relationship between theory and experience? School trains you to be a spectator in life, never a participant.

The separation of knowledge and experience has massive consequences. Some have knowledge and never a clue on how to apply it. Some have the courage to live but —with their brain firmly in a wheelchair—have never learned how to learn. There's all kinds of statistics about people who do not read after they leave school but we don't even need the statistics, just go talk to people. You'll find many don't read. Many get comfortable with where they are at. And why shouldn't they? They're already *educated,* at least according to that paper hanging on the wall. In some sense, I can't blame them. By forcing people to learn a lifetime's worth of meaningless nonsense, school murders the love they have for learning. Having been told their whole life that jumping through the hoops to the piece of paper means "educated", they now believe themselves to be educated. The massive growth of the self-help industry over the last century is a testament to school's utter failure to equip individuals to help themselves.

It's no coincidence that many successful people in the world have dropped out of school. They're not geniuses or crazy exceptions to some rule of success. They figured out before everyone else that school is a massive waste of time, compared with creating something real in the world or going out into the world to learn from people who know.

If what you learn in school is not applicable in your life, it's worthless. If it has no worth, it has no meaning.

Should the future janitor learn physics? Should the lawyer learn art? Should the mathematician learn biology? Should the musician learn anatomy?

Education is invaluable and unending. If a janitor wants to learn physics, they absolutely should. But why should society force them? By forcing physics on children, if they aren't particularly motivated, we kill much of the future potential kids have for the love of physics. The understanding of physics is useful, but exactly how useful is it? How many working professionals use physics? Is physics so useful that all children *must be forced* to learn it, or else their future prospects will be compromised? or worse, ruined?

Any person has their entire life to learn physics. Instead of teaching kids to read and then setting them free in the library of the world, we whack them over the head with books they are forced to read (with book reports, essays and tests following). I'd certainly read much fewer books now if I was trying to write nonsensical reports and take tests after each one, and not just because of all the time wasted on frivolous exercises. The love of reading—the love of learning—is murdered before the child steps a single foot into the literary playground of the world.

If I wanted people to stop reading, I wouldn't forbid it. I'd force children into a terrible experience with reading and they'll spend a lifetime avoiding books. In the same way you could force a child to eat broccoli once a day for twelve years and they'll likely hate broccoli for the rest of their lives. Few people are forced into something they later enjoy. By thumping children repeatedly over the head with seminal works of literature, is it any surprise that more than half of all adults in this country spend their lives avoiding serious reading? A horrible experience does more damage to future prospects than anything else.

Cevin Soling poetically wrote in a recent article on Forbes.com:

> "All of school pathologies make sense when you understand that people – which include children – do not enjoy or respond well to being subjected to a repressive environment. While it is possible for a North Korean POW to learn calculus under duress from their prison guard, it is reasonable to assume they will: A) associate math with incarceration; B) despise the inmates who learn for appearing readily complicit with their captors; and C) try to *forget* the information the moment they are free. Sound familiar?"

In addition to taught logical and philosophical observations against school, technology has made school obsolete. All resources gained within school are readily—and cheaply—available outside. Thanks to the internet, one has access to experts in all fields, across the globe. Libraries and the internet have brought all the information in the world—at almost no cost—to the feet of any who would pick it up. Since the resources in school are now redundant, school is little more than a babysitting service. How much more could children learn if they were set free in the world? How much work could they accomplish for themselves in the time they would be drilled with meaningless math or propagandized history?

The obvious counter argument is that students wouldn't be motivated to learn on their own. What intelligent person would be excited to learn worthless technical information, at the expense of anything useful? Are children unmotivated because they are forced into a hostile environment from when they are very young? Or are children naturally unmotivated?

I've learned more in the last few years of personal study —thanks to motivation and available information—than in all of my years in school buildings. I *want* to learn, so I learn much faster, remember much more, and use much of it; unlike school where learning was sluggish, I have forgotten most of what was covered, and don't use hardly —if any—of what remains.

To mask rampant intellectual and economic failings— along with obsolescence—school issues degrees or diplomas; official certification. The degree is official proof of a knowledge or skill and the stated goal in society has become ever more education for everyone (which means more degrees). The unfortunates of society suffer from a "lack of education (school)". So it turns out, we use the degree as a form of protectionism. If you don't have the degree, you get withheld from various avenues in society, regardless of your ability to learn, your character, or qualities. People realize this, so they advocate for all kinds of scholarships or ways to make "access" to schooling fair and equal (solving surplus through addition). You know what answer the "educators" never come up with? Removing degrees/diplomas altogether. If degrees weren't (typically) required for upward mobility (ex: many jobs now require a degree for promotion), the lack of a degree wouldn't hold the disadvantaged-but-motivated back. Upward mobility would rest in much larger part with the individual, rather than on their ability to play the system, or become indentured to it.

Schools could never tolerate to remove the degree. Then you'd have to be paying schools to learn skills, and since schools teach as few useful skills as possible (as evidenced by the teachers' lack of experience in every field and unknown factor of what technical skills each child needs), people wouldn't pay. Under the illusion of "education", the piece of paper is a magnificent scam to get people to pay a boatload of money, and waste years of their lives, and even go into debt for...a piece of paper. You can watch college classes for free on television. You can buy their textbooks cheaply (used) or even attend various lectures for free. The internet has made information easily accessible; often free. Even getting important contacts in the world is a simple matter of contacting people. Yet, no matter how smart you are, how intelligent, how much you know, what you can do, how high quality of a person you are...if you don't fork over the cash for the paper, society at large has decided that you will be ostracized. You are automatically disqualified from various jobs. You are denied promotion ("it's the policy"). You are referred to as (and therefore assumed to be) "uneducated".

The reality is that you have to buy the paper because a bunch of suckers already bought the paper. Talk to some of the kids with the paper who are looking for jobs now about their college experience; half of them seem to have majored in beer pong. A really expensive piece of paper and years of beer pong are the literal requirements to be considered fit to join society. Since few people could be rationally talked into enslaving themselves and wasting their lives—so long as it's dressed up as a "diploma" and "education", and so long as the clients have spent the last twelve years of their lives being brainwashed—the ruse works. Spend years ensuring that children understand the emperor has the most magnificent clothes and you have no worries when he shows up naked. They've grown up believing.

This is the root of the emotional fortress around school. School *has* to be valuable, otherwise a person has worked so hard for...what?

A sham. Who wants to admit they worked hard for a sham? Who wants to admit they went into debt for an illusion? Who wants to admit that the framed piece of paper and years of their life have amounted to a pittance of the perceived value? Unfortunately for all of us with degrees, all of us who have been to school, whether or not we admit we've been hoodwinked has nothing to do with the fact that we have been.

Who should decide what children have to learn? Who should set the curriculum? Who (outside parents) can decide what another human should be required to know before they are allowed to live? Hurdles they must jump before they are allowed a fair shake at life in the world? You've heard it a thousand times over, "if you don't get an *education...*" then your life is going to be horrible (or some other variation on this typical response). Says who? Who sets the curriculum? Who requires children to go to school?

The government. Under the stated intent of "the good of society", or the noble aim of "education" or "an educated society", and the violent arm of the law; the government requires children to go to school (via various state laws), and sets the curricula in public schools. In private schools, curricula is set by the school, but in most cases closely follows public schools as the state of California says, "Private high schools have the authority to set their own graduation requirements. However, many private high schools do include at least the state minimum courses in order to ensure that students transitioning to or from public schools have less disruption in their progress toward graduation."

Is there any doubt that the government has a vested interest in directing people to think certain things in certain ways?

Here's a little history lesson you never learned in school. The man considered the father of public schooling in the United States is Horace Mann (who bizarrely claimed "The State is the father of children."). He discovered the school system used by the Prussians, thought it was excellent, brought it to the United States, and spearheaded it's legal implemented here. Our schools are based on the old Prussian model.

Prussian schools were created after Prussia's defeat by Napoleon. In analyzing their defeat, Prussia decided soldiers on the field of battle were thinking independently. They designed a free, compulsory eight year course that trained students in rudimentary skills to be fit for the industrial revolution, but also trained them to be disciplined, obedient soldiers. Above all, authority and obedience was paramount. The purpose of Prussian schools was to drill conformity and obedience into children.

Johann Gottlieb Fichte, the German philosopher who had a profound impact on the Prussian school system upon which our current system is based is quoted:

> "Education should aim at destroying free will so that after pupils are thus schooled they will be incapable throughout the rest of their lives of thinking or acting otherwise than as their school masters would have wished...when the technique has been perfected, every government that has been in charge of education for more than one generation will be able to control it's subjects securely without the need of armies or policemen."

Do you understand the implication? If people started to think for themselves, they might try to start acting for themselves. People who are capable of thinking and acting for themselves must come to the inevitable conclusion that government is, at best, a superfluous middleman; typically, a sham; and at its worst, a plague against humanity.

The reason we require government is because people are generally incapable of self-governance. The first step toward making governance acceptable is to convince each person mentally and emotionally that they are unfit for self-governance. Even better, don't bring it up. Present government as if it was the only possible option (the general alternative is chaos and destruction). Out of sight, out of mind.

It couldn't possibly be that people are unaware of the concept of self-governance because they're taught much of what they know about governance in a government monopolized school system, could it? It couldn't have anything to do with a schooling system where we are brought up with a general reverence for the government's history, heroes, and ideals, could it? It's a conflict of interest to be in the business of controlling people, teaching them that they don't need to be controlled.

The prime interests of school and government are *the interests of school and government.* Control, authority, servility, ignorance, compliance and obedience.

As a simple, obvious example, in school the child is never led to question the validity of school itself, even as a thought experiment. For the sake of it's own survival (and the self-esteem of all who have a stake in the game), school cannot lead you to question school itself. How quickly would (the illusion of) schools fall apart if schools debated the merits of school inside the classroom? Much in the same way you will never hear an official government discourse on the legitimacy of government. The emperor must remain clothed in our minds to ensure that we behave as if he is clothed and the easiest way to make sure minds stay corralled is to never open the gate.

The government cannot teach children how the economy really works, because that would require children to learn how they are enslaved and defrauded for their entire lives. School cannot teach people about all the better ways they can learn about living outside of school because they would educate themselves right out of a job. So the first lessons of school, in the interests of government and school; slavery is freedom and obedience is education.

School destroys children. Observe five year-old children. At five years old, they're curious, spontaneous, adventurous, motivated, willing, excitable, and strong personalities. On the other end of school, many kids are now depressed, bored, cynical, burned out, apathetic, and medicated. How is it that we manage to stamp out many of the best qualities in a person in their formative years?

This is all without mentioning the escalating similarities between schools and prisons. Children walking through metal detectors or being searched. Children arrested for "crimes", such as putting on perfume. Increasing numbers of children leaving school with criminal records. It only facilitates obedience and compliance with authority; ruining the lives of many children in the process.

School doesn't educate kids. School teaches kids to conform. School teaches kids to think well within the box. School teaches kids to hate many interesting facets of life by repetitively, meaninglessly, mercilessly beating them over the head with them.

The only way I know of to measure a person's ability *to think* is to experience them; to see them solve a problem, speak with them about the world, or work together with them. The education of a person *cannot be measured with grades and pieces of paper.*

If it seems like I am angry, I'm not. I'm furious! I am absolutely incensed that a million well-meaning, good-intentioned people get duped into doing the exact opposite of what they intend. I know teachers; there are some in my family. I don't hate the people, I hate the schools. I hate what schools have done to people. Education is the hope for the future, but we actively destroy this hope on a daily basis through the institution of school.

As a parent, I don't understand why you would want a teacher taught teacher to teach your kids how to be exactly the same as all the other kids who are held to the lowest possible level (and it has to be the lowest possible level. Any standard broad enough to cover millions of students is going to be lousy enough to cover millions of students. More on this later). You're blessed with a young life to guide into the world and you'd ship them off to have somebody else cultivate their mind? You'd willingly hand off the highest responsibilities of a parent—to set the foundations of a young life—to a random stranger?

I don't blame the kids. I feel tremendously sorry for them. It makes me furious that we, as a society, seem to agree that this system of destruction is acceptable. Worse, most people seem to froth at the mouth with excitement when it comes to schooling.

It is acceptable to crush young personalities before they can bloom. It is acceptable to press brains into tight containers. It is acceptable to bend a beautiful spirit to fit the yolk of repetitious obedience. It is acceptable to pressure future generations into indenturing themselves to banking institutions before they find their own way in the world.

If you would ever wish to discover what is possible in life, the last place I would ever wish you to find yourself would be in a school.

CURRENCY MONOPOLY

Hundreds of years ago, you may have used your skills to produce surplus value. Your apple orchard produced extra apples and you are hungry for some meat. You've got to find someone who raises meat to barter with; see if you can't trade some of those extra apples for some meat. It's not an easy task. Assuming you find somebody with meat to trade, how do you know if they will want apples? How will they divide the meat up in a way to trade for an appropriate amount of apples? Having a few extra apples doesn't necessarily mean that somebody will slaughter a whole animal to trade with you. Surplus goods are no guarantee of barter.

This is how currency (money) comes about. Currency is a medium of exchange. One of the original currencies was salt. You'd trade your apples for some salt. You can trade your salt for some meat. The man with meat can trade his meat for salt, and then exchange salt for your apples. Salt was widely used and is easily divisible. Salt is not ideal though, because it is easily consumed or destroyed. Over time, better currencies arise naturally. Eventually, precious metals became currency; gold and silver in particular, due to their relative indestructibility and ease of division. Alternative currencies pop up when the need arises, much how soldiers in WW2 traded cigarettes with each other.

Nowadays, currencies are not commodities that you can trade in the market, nor are they representative of commodities (such as a dollar representing a pound of salt or an ounce of gold). Currencies are now fiat currencies; pieces of paper indicating a value set by the issuing government/bank. When salt was money, salt had a value of it's own. It was worth something on it's own, aside from being a medium of exchange. The paper dollars we carry around now have no value of their own. Without a government decreeing value, they would be worth, literally, a piece of paper. If you had a bag of salt, it would have a particular value to all people, across time. If you had an American dollar, how many people over the course of history would care? The dollar has no intrinsic value.

Fiat currencies—currencies based on stated value—are absolutely destructive to the average citizen because citizens end up getting taxed at least twice. By keeping control of the money, the government can take what it wants through overt taxation and then take more through inflation. A currency monopoly is a direct attack on the very poorest in society; the less money you have, the more vulnerable you are to theft and manipulation.

Does anyone (except for those running them) not understand that monopolies are bad? In the marketplace, a company with a monopoly in the marketplace can fix the price, reduce supply, arbitrarily decrease the quality; in short—take advantage of the consumer. It is easy to lament the ills of a monopoly in the marketplace, but is the government monopoly any different?

We value products and services such as taking care of the elderly, long-term investment accounts, paved roads, making sure citizens are not using violence on one another, or eating nontoxic food. Yet, the government taxes everyone in order to pay for valuable things that might otherwise come about naturally in the marketplace. This is all under the guise that *maybe* somebody would go without, or *for the good of society.* And yet, even in the best of government programs, many still go without and the services that are rendered are of the least possible quality. One of the huge problems with government programs is that the results rarely lead to self-sufficiency, without which, the programs must go on indefinitely;

taxing more resources from society. If government programs solved a problem, they would plan for their own obsolescence once it is solved.

The obvious logical flaw: if government programs worked, we would need less of them. If government programs reduced poverty, we would need less continuing government programs to continue reducing poverty. If government made us safer, we would need less government to continue to make us safer. If the government did what it claims to do, we would need less government. If government created peace, we would need less military and aggression, because the world would be more peaceful. That the government continually balloons in size is precise evidence that it completely fails at the stated intentions. Or...maybe the stated intentions aren't the real intentions?

Once you're free from the confines of school, you can go to work. You've got to make the money (especially if you've got a daunting student loan). Except, it's not just *making* the money; you've got to keep *making increasingly more* money. It's not good enough to just make money. A natural life progression is one of the factors requiring the making of more money; people have families. That's nothing to write home about; as you require more resources you must acquire more resources.

But you must also acquire more resources because whatever resources you have accumulated are constantly being taken from you. Even if you had a large lump sum of money, theoretically large enough to live out your life on, you'd still have to account for taxes and inflation. Taxes and inflation, through a monopoly on the currency, are methods used to funnel wealth upwards while maintaining (and increasing) control.

This is where it starts to get confusing, people get divided against each other, and a thousand different "experts" will show up with a million different opinions.....

Inevitably, the government spends more money this year than they spent last year. This isn't an absolute but it's about as close as we can come to one. The last time the government didn't have a deficit or debt, none of us were alive, and a chart showing the increases in government spending is easily found. The money has to come from somewhere.

In part, it comes from taxes.

> "The power to tax involves the power to destroy."
> -John Marshall, fourth Chief Justice of the Supreme Court

Taxes fill the government account. Most government spending is either wasted or used to further control. Almost by default, government expenditures must be a waste since governments have very few productive options to spend the money on. It is not as easily understood that taxes also serve as protectionism. Taxes deter competition. Taxes make it easier for those with more money to keep power and control.

Why does the government's account need to be filled by taxes? The government cannot fill it's account without taxes because it does not produce goods and services to exchange for value in a marketplace.

Businesses, unlike governments, create value. Businesses that do not create value are no longer in business (or they're bailed out and subsidized by the government). Businesses create a good or service, the good or service has a value, and people exchange them another value (typically money) for the good or service. The reason why government has to forcibly remove your money from you is because you would not voluntarily pay for their products or services. The government has to take what they fail to earn. Who would voluntarily put money into Social Security?

A monopoly on currency allows for a straightforward method of taxing. Income and sales taxes are both straightforward. As you make money—right off the top—the government takes a piece. Sales tax is similar, only the government takes a portion of the top of a business transaction.

The most overtly destructive tax is property tax; typically an annual percentage of assessed property value. Owning land is one of the premier ways to become self-sufficient. Property tax ensures that it becomes increasingly difficult for an individual to become self-sufficient; always needing to pay rent to the landlords. It's not enough to purchase the land, you must work enough to continue to pay rent on it.

In addition to thievery, taxes serve as a hurdle; limiting competition. If taxes on businesses are higher, it is harder to start businesses. If it's harder to start new businesses, there will be less businesses; less competition. Established businesses—while they may not like paying more taxes—make more money by maintaining a larger section of their industry due to less competition. Less competition allows them greater power over money and markets tomorrow; not just increased money today.

If taxes increase as you make more money, it becomes harder to accumulate wealth as your earnings increase. "Progressive" taxes put downward pressure on social mobility. An economic caste system is hardly a "progressive" idea.

So far, I have been using the term "taxes" literally, but there is another indirect tax. One of the largest, invisible ways we are taxed is through inflation. If you talk to the average person, inflation seems to be this mysterious force

—a law of nature—causing the inevitable rising price of goods and services (complete ignorance on everyday issues such as this are a shining tribute to public school). Inflation is only tolerable through ignorance. Inflation is deliberate; inflation is a tax; and inflation is evil. Inflation funnels money upward without ever having to touch the money. Worse, the poorer you are, the harder you are hit by inflation.

Inflation can happen for multiple subtle reasons in natural ways, such as changes in supply and demand. Unfortunately, much of the inflation we experience now is not due to subtle workings of natural economy but through the expansion of the money supply (printing money).

Imagine you and I are the only people on the planet. Our total economy is worth $2 and we each have a one dollar bill, representing half of the economy. We each have half of all the purchasing power; $1. Now let's say that I print one more dollar for myself (I now have $2, you have $1).

Nothing has happened with the value of our economy—it is still only valued at two total dollars—but the value is now represented with three $1 bills. Only the monetary representation (number of dollars) has changed in our economy, but I have increased my purchasing power, my total value. Each of the three dollars, in our two dollar economy, now represents 66 cents (33%) of purchasing power (out of the $2 total). By printing myself another dollar, I increased how much value I have! I have two dollars, or 66% of the money (representing $1.33 of our $2 economy). Your purchasing power, with your single dollar, is now worth 67 cents. *Printing money changed our wealth. I printed money and became richer at your expense! And I did it without your knowledge or consent!*

The value in our economy didn't change so everything still has the same total worth of two dollars (represented by three dollars). Since I only changed the money, the medium of value exchange, then the price of everything would adjust as well; prices will go up. Something that used to cost $1, half of all the value that exists, would now cost $1.50, and I will have two dollars. You only have a single dollar. I now have a financial advantage over you by manipulating the medium of exchange.

Manipulation is the name of the game now, thanks to the Federal Reserve. Cleverly named, the Federal Reserve is a private bank; the private bank that controls the money supply of the country. Let me repeat: *a private bank has a monopoly on our currency.* As the Federal Reserve prints money and hands it out to their banker/corporate/government friends, or random foreign countries, the total money supply is increased. Value is created at the top; the new money is first spent by those blessed by the central bank (their friends and friendly governments). As the money supply increases, value is automatically shifted to accommodate those new dollars; prices must go up. Inflation allows the banks to create wealth at the top for governments and their friends, while impoverishing *everyone at the bottom with* cash; all without their knowing or understanding! Inflation assures that—even outside of direct taxation—wealth will always be flowing upward through the shifting value!

> "The monopoly of a single bank is certainly an evil."
> -Thomas Jefferson

It almost sounds too fantastic to be true, but rudimentary research will show you the facts. A central bank controls our money and keeps a steady, hidden stream of money always flowing toward the top, not by taking your dollars, but by printing (which mostly consists of adding numbers in computer accounts) themselves more dollars. I won't even get into how the money is misused through fractional-reserve banking.

> "It is well enough that people of the nation do not understand our banking and money system, for if they did, I believe there would be a revolution before tomorrow morning." -Henry Ford

At this point I always ask myself, how could anyone get away with this? That's a lot of stealing (taxes)! Aside from the obvious answer that "we continue to allow it", the currency monopoly for three reasons. First, our wealth has increased a tremendous amount thanks to technological advances and the passage of time. Technology has allowed us to increase the speed at which we accumulate value. If done subtly, governments can skim off the top without much notice. It works even better if governments can convince you that it is normal, or even certain, that you will be taxed. You'll begin to welcome the opportunity to *do your duty.* As fools say, "That's just the price of belonging to a society."

Second, the death-of-a-thousand-paper-cuts. They break it up into many tiny, barely-noticeable bits. If they just took 60+% of everyone's money, all hell would break loose. But if they take 25% of your income off the top, 8% of every purchase, another 5% on your property, 5% on top of all the gasoline or alcohol (in addition to other luxury taxes) you buy, a series of meaningless "registrations" (marriage, car, etc), devalue the currency 10% a year, you've lost a sizable portion of your money without being fully cognizant of how thoroughly you've been fleeced. Before long, half of your income is gone, if not more.

The Cost of Government Center[2] calculates a "Cost of Government Day", which is the day marking when the average American would have earned enough to pay for his/her share of government spending and regulatory burdens. Cost of Government Day fell on August 12th in

---

2 http://www.costofgovernment.org/

2011. Every cent earned by the average American from January 1st to August 12th in 2011 went toward costs imposed upon them by their own government.

The third reason that government can get away with so much taxation is the same reason why government gets away with everything. Violence. If you don't like it, too bad. They can throw you in jail. They can shoot you. They can make a law that says they can shoot you. They can make a law that says they can't shoot you, and then shoot you anyway ("qualified immunity"). Ironically, should your dispute with the government end up in one of the government's courts, they'll use the money you've been paying them to fight against whatever money you might have left to pursue your case in court.

Ultimately, backing the currency monopoly is a monopoly on violence. Pay your taxes or thugs show up at your house with guns and take you to jail. People don't pay their taxes because they'd like to. People pay their taxes because they are under the threat of personal injury or death. The monopoly on currency assures that your transactions can be kept track of for proper taxing, the monopoly assures that wealth will always be flowing upward, it assures that governments will always have more money to waste, and it assures that you, your family, your friends, and your community will always be on the blunt end of theft. Any value stored in a monopolized currency will always be manipulated, leading to the destruction of value for the benefit of those running the currency. The lowest wage-earners in the country are the hardest hit by the monopoly on currency.

MITIGATING RISK

(It's a dangerous world, after all.)
(Oh...and guaranteeing profits, too.)
(aaaaand subsidizing irresponsibility.....shhhh)

When banks print money, it's not merely enough to print the money and hold it. Having money doesn't really make you any richer. If you work for minimum wage, win the lottery, blow the money on fancy stuff or let it sit in the bank, and still only have 8 bucks an hour coming in, you're not much richer. Rich people understand a pile of money doesn't make you rich; streams of income make you rich.

Bankers need streams of income to keep the money flowing upward toward them. They achieve this through lending money and receiving the principle plus interest in return. To some degree, lending money is normal; a certain amount of financed capital will naturally take place. However—driven by the pressures of profits, performance, and greed—when accountability (consequences) is removed, bankers are able to force much more phony wealth into the market to increase the streams of income coming their way. Having the money to give away isn't enough—they could lose it overnight—they need a vehicle to protect themselves against massive loss.

Lending newly printed money to people who have no increase in wealth is a substantial risk; how would they pay it back if they were to lose it? What if the house burned down? What if the car crashed? What if they were to get ill? The other side of the coin that allows the rich to get richer (and has created an entire new host of people who have gotten rich off of the business itself) is designed to mitigate irresponsibility, risk, and occasionally misfortune at the expense of productive, responsible people. We call this scheme *insurance.*

All insurance operates under the same ponzi scheme; more responsible people must be included to offset the irresponsible. Healthy people are required to insure sick people. Good drivers are required to insure bad drivers. People who live in temperate places are required to insure the fools who build houses in the path of devastating hurricanes every few years. Living people are required to insure the family of the deceased.

On a basic level, insurance is just a matter of paying in the present to avoid paying in the future. However, the unwritten assumption is that everyone will not be paying in the future. If everyone got into a car crash tomorrow, that would be the end of the auto insurance industry.

Unfortunately, the avoidance of consequences in the future is exactly the thing that keeps people from making bad decisions in the present. If we remove consequences, people are making decisions (and banks and insurance companies are making profits) in the present that will hurt them all the way into the future. Insurance becomes a subsidization of irresponsible decision-making.

Both parties make foolish decisions because of insurance. The buyer gets compensated if they do something stupid (or in a rare case of misfortune). The bank has guaranteed collateral.

Insurance distorts reality—in the mind first—leading us to believe we live in a world with little-to-no consequences. Back to my analogy on accountability, there's a reason people don't wander out onto freeways (and animals do); they're aware of the risk and consequence of being hit by a quickly moving vehicle. If people could somehow be made unaware of the results of being hit by a vehicle on the freeway, we'd have as many human carcasses on the side of the road as animals. Removing consequences from consideration only furthers the likelihood that they will happen, since the consequence itself is the deterrent.

Because insurance is available (or worse, required), individuals make irresponsible decisions they wouldn't otherwise make. With insurance, banks lend much more money than they otherwise would. The insurance guarantees that—in the event of catastrophe to the collateral—banks will have some sort of return on investment. If the bank's money was more easily subjected to real world loss (due to the irresponsibility of the borrower, acts of theft, or catastrophe), the banks would be much more cautious about whom they lent money to.

Because insurance is available (or required), people are more likely to buy the car/house that they cannot afford. If it were to be damaged or destroyed, it is essentially replaced. A man making $30,000 a year doesn't have to hesitate to buy a $20,000 car. The bank makes the profit or repossesses the car. Insurance retains the profits for the bank, while making sure that the individual doesn't lose the purchase that they couldn't afford in the first place.

Financing spreads the purchase across future years while putting money in the banker's pockets. Insurance guarantees the bank's profits while cutting a portion off the top for themselves. Irresponsible people have their assets replaced. Responsible people foot the bill.

Without insurance, would banks finance massive houses across the country? Without insurance, would individuals agree to be indebted for houses and cars they couldn't afford? Without insurance, would individuals consider the costs of taking care of their own health? Wouldn't the cost of medical care be significantly reduced?

I have no doubt that insurance is directly responsible for the irresponsible driving of the average person. Why do we not consider the gravity of driving thousands of tons of metal and glass at high speeds? Because we rarely face the consequences of doing so, until they become severe. Insurance distorts the consequences of driving a vehicle. With insurance, all consequences are reduced to the cost of the deductible (or the minor traffic fine), until the coverage is exceeded (rare), or death.

If you get into a minor scrape in the car, you pay a small amount, or the deductible. If you get into a decent wreck, you pay the deductible. If you total the car, you pay the deductible. Other than potential personal harm (which seems unlikely since all we hear about on commercials is the safety excellence of every car), the costs are the same. The consequences of a minor scrape and smashing into another vehicle are oftentimes the same; why would anyone consider the serious costs when there likely won't be any?

And this is how texting-while-driving goes from being a minor fine to being a death sentence. Irresponsible drivers —who would usually be involved in a series of escalating incidences—would be too poor, or out of a vehicle, to continue driving in the face of escalating consequences; they'd be unable to smash into the responsible driver who otherwise subsidizes their irresponsibility through insurance. Why would anyone be inclined to consider the risks? We force them (through mandatory auto insurance) to eliminate most of the risks through a monthly payment.

Is it any surprise that we live in a culture of irresponsibility? We force responsible people to assume much of the consequences of the irresponsible; allowing them to flourish. Bad drivers continue having cars to drive. Stupid people keep building new houses in hurricane zones. Unhealthy people feel little pressure to change their lifestyles. And for the few misfortuned, there's more than enough private charity that would happily help.

I imagine that much of what I've written in the last two chapters might not resonate with the average American. We seem like a prosperous society. It seems like many people have money. How can the banksters (and their friends) be robbing our country blind if we all have so much? And that's the problem; insurance has enabled the illusion of wealth to grow.

If the amount of wealth a person has is directly related to the amount they earn then it would be a simple thing to measure our worth. But it isn't so simple anymore. Over the last hundred years, those on top of the game have replaced real wealth with an illusion. We have transferred from an expansion of wealth to an expansion of credit (debt) and insurance. So it may seem on the surface that more people can afford fancy cars and expensive houses, but the reality is that more people can *go into debt* for fancy cars and expensive houses. I have yet to encounter an economic argument that counts a car *payment* as an asset.

The easy financing is backed by insurance, which ensures that the price of cars and homes aren't lowered to affordable standards. Supply and demand being the basic driver of price, a raising demand means that the price will stay higher. Demand will always be greater as the price lowers, so businesses have the incentive to find ways to lower prices (cutting operational costs, new technology, etc). But what if we could find ways to maintain artificially high demand? Prices wouldn't have to come down, and everyone would benefit (except for the consumer).

Insurance on $500,000 houses allows more people to borrow money for the house, meaning there isn't incentive for builders to figure out better, cheaper ways to build that $500,000 house. Insurance subsidizes irresponsibility of largess, propping up demand to an artificial height (it's not that more people can afford the house, but more people can now go into debt for the house since the bank's investment is protected by insurance), which in turn makes *all* houses more expensive. Every consumer suffers increased prices while businesses, banks, and insurance companies make exponential profits on top of the pyramid.

Individuals are encouraged to indenture themselves to the banksters while insurance cartels make a killing on the backs of the productive and responsible. The fraudulence of banks and politicians is becoming much more widely known and accepted, but it is little understood how insurance fits into the scheme. Banks print the money. Insurance companies make sure they maintain profits. Politicians make sure the whole scheme remains “legal” and police make sure their neighbors comply.

LAW MONOPOLY

Law and government are two different vehicles. The diversification of evil is genius in this way; in many centuries past, when one man was responsible as king—legislator, prophet, judge, and jury—people knew who to get mad at; they knew where to strike when it came time to rebel. There's an entire lineage of kings and emperors overthrown by angry populaces and armies. Under a giant bureaucracy, with a vast number of representatives, a panel of sacred judges, a president, and a library of laws that nobody can read, it would seem like nobody is responsible for the ills in our society. In part, it's a fair estimation, no one man is entirely responsible. Diversification has slowed the pace of evil and diffused responsibility but it is important to realize that the idea cuts both ways; it also makes positive change exceptionally difficult, if not impossible.

The division of law and government is important. A monopoly on law—facilitated by monopolies on land and violence—gives (seemingly) legitimate authority to government. Government appears to be legitimate under the foundation of law and law derives it's legitimacy through land and violence.

The (alleged) ownership of land creates a jurisdiction. If the law didn't own the land, how could it tell a foreign landowner what to do? The (alleged) justification to use violence gives it weight. If the law cannot physically force a person to comply, it wouldn't have much effective weight.

Since governments derive their legitimacy from law, corrupt governments must stem from corrupt laws. Wouldn't a just law, properly enforced, restrict corruption?

Problems of government stem from problems of law. Law itself has a clever hierarchy; city law superseded by county law, county law by state law, and state law by federal law. So many masters, so many rules, so much confusion, but the root of our legal problems can be traced to the law that governs the others; federal law. No matter the changes on the city, county, or state level if the federal government can force you to do the opposite (as people who have had their dispensaries raided by federal troops when they have state permits have found out). If law is to be addressed, it must be addressed at the top; the federal level.

Any attempt to address government without addressing law (and it's enforcement) is merely rearranging deck chairs on the Titanic; it will amount to nothing. Worse, it is a waste of valuable time. So much of the system is designed around tricking people into addressing governance without addressing the roots of many problems; the monopolization of land and violence.

The Supreme Court is used as a (mental and emotional) legitimizer of last resort, but the verdict is usually the same; government employees in black robes rule in favor of the government. Elections merely put new people into office, but leave the entire system unscathed. Various people throughout our history are lauded for humanitarian victories—such as Martin Luther King Jr.—but the systems in place that created (and are still creating) the exploitation they fought remain just as they were. Monopolies on law and government—land and violence—which exploit the entire population, remain wholly intact.

> "A man is no less a slave because he is allowed to choose a new master once in a term of years."
> -Lysander Spooner

People know—especially in modern times—there is a difference between what is *right* and what is law. Our history—all of human history—is filled with peoples fighting against unjust laws. The indigenous people of this country, poor whites, blacks, minorities, and women have all been on the overtly unjust end of laws.

If you try to study law and governance, you are likely to run up against a nonsensical Gordian Knot. As Alexander of Macedonia discovered, complexity is the illusionary gatekeeper designed to keep out the feeble-minded. There's all kinds of legal theory or legal philosophy. There's an entire industry that makes up the law; another that "practices" law. Formalities. Precedence. Legal-speak. It's all designed around (or to disguise) the simple fact that a "law" is a rule written on a piece of paper.

In various older times, there has been legal theory based on Natural Rights. A system of law based around the sovereignty of the individual and the locality of the procedure (meaning, you commit a crime in your neighborhood, it is the people in your neighborhood who decide and dispense justice) can be just, and there is all sorts of ideas based around those concepts. However, concepts of Natural Law, principles of logic (innocent until proven guilty), or even Constitutionality (if it ever was valid) have now been tossed out the window. What we are left with is rules of monopolized cartels writing whatever they want and calling it "law".

> "But rightful liberty is unobstructed action according to our will within limits drawn around us by the equal rights of others. I do not add "within the limits of the law," because law is often but the tyrant's will, and always so when it violates the right of an individual."
> -Thomas Jefferson

Laws in this country aren't based on principles, laws are based on the opinions of those writing them. Not only that, but the same group of friends writes the law, passes the law, enforces the law, and then dispenses justice based on the law. It's a monopoly, and a conflict of interest to do anything (more than minimally required) for the masses, since anything promoting the freedom and power of the individual is in direct contrast to the superiority and sovereignty of the State.

It takes a single reading of "The Law" by Frederic Bastiat to realize that laws are not made on any moral principle; but in a manner for politicians and their friends to exploit all others. Even better—thanks to the knot our minds have been tied into, and the emotional manipulations built around law—rulers are able to get away with the game as neighbors argue with each other. It is always a sad day for those in charge when exploited people realize their plight, so efforts of control are largely designed around maintaining an ignorant, divided population.

I want to repeat for emphasis: a law is a rule written down on paper (with "representatives" giving the illusion of "consent"). When this country was formed, the founders agreed on the Constitution. They wrote it down on a piece of paper and signed it. Previously, The Declaration of Independence and Articles of Confederation; written on paper and signed. All the way to current times, we could fill entire museums with rules written onto paper. Laws can be valid, but laws require a couple conditions in order to validate them.

First, a law must come from a legitimate authority. Laws of science, as an example, are based on realities of the natural world. Natural Laws are based on the reality of our experience. Being born free doesn't require an explanation, it is easily observable every time a child is born. Freedom of speech is simply understood; we are born free and with mouths. Reality is the authority which validates these laws. Conversely, laws of government are created in a very magical, ceremonious kind of way so as to presume the validation of authority. In reality, none exists. Or rather, the authority is not natural; it is produced artificially. This is the original ideal behind governments of old. You'll never question God, so if the king is God, or the voice of God...

Second, (without an authentic authority) a law requires consent. Our government has no supernatural, or even natural authority over anyone. They can only govern by the consent of the citizens. Our Declaration of Independence says, "Governments are instituted among Men, deriving their just powers from the consent of the governed..." Government understands it's own limitation, so they construct a giant artificial pony-show around our subjection to make it seem official, authoritative, natural, or even supernatural; to seem as if our consent has already been had.

We now vote for *representatives* (who represent themselves and their moneyed friends) who go about passing laws *in our name. They represent us* (as the story goes). Have you consented? Has anyone consented? Or were we all born with little other choice? So long as nobody argues to the contrary, we can all just assume we're being represented. We assume that, like gravity, there is no other possible outcome and nothing could be further from the truth.

If I were to come over to your house, I would have to respect your house rules; the laws of the house. It's your house, you can make the rules. Nobody is forcing me to come for a visit. If I do not like the rules, I can leave. What would happen if you tried to enforce your house rules at my house? Yet, somehow we are convinced into continue to appoint *representatives* to enforce their house rules in our house. The manipulation of words is powerful. If they tell us they are "representing" us, and that they are doing it for the "good of society", it takes genuine mental dexterity (which you have likely been robbed of during school) to unpack all the manipulation.

Actual servants of times past (you know, the ones who walked around emptying the master's bedpan) would probably not consider their servitude to be very noble but then, they didn't lord over the household—they were themselves lorded over. Kings didn't saunter around calling themselves the "servant" of the slaves as they do today.

Modern day slave masters have adopted the language to confuse us, calling themselves "servants". Rather than think of them much more accurately as "oligarchs", "gangsters", or "tyrants", thinking of them as "public servants" placates your own mind and lulls you into obedience. "They're serving the public!" A simple exercise in logic reveals the house of cards that the wind of free thought blows into oblivion.

We allow the farce of an unjust legal system for three reasons. The first two reasons: an emotional protection built around law (notice how many people talk about the Constitution) and a severe manipulation of language.

Respect the Law. Law of the land. Justice is blind. We have a strong emotional attachment to *doing right* and we have been conditioned to believe that the faulty laws of faulty men are, with rare exception, *right.* We might each have various opinions as to certain laws, but as far as *the law* goes, you will rarely hear a gripe. It's a clever shell game; so long as you're focused on finding the unlawful pea, you'll never realize the whole game is stacked. Courtrooms filled with legal shills keep the game going. A society of ever changing laws will always end in compromise, corruption, and violent extortion.

We've manipulated the language of and around the word "law". Law has become synonymous with "justice", "authority", "morality", and "right"; all to the benefit of *law* and those controlling it, of course. If a court should rule in a particular way—moral principles be damned—

right has been redefined and all must fall into suit. It's *the law,* after all (and you have to feel good that justice has been served). The wording used around law serves to reinforce good feelings about *law,* even if particular laws are unlawful, or nearly all of our legal system is in direct defiance of Natural Law.

The third reason why we allow a crooked monopoly of law is simple; it is backed by the monopoly of violence. What can you do in the face of somebody who is (supposedly) *allowed* to kill you? Not much, really. Even less if you are disarmed, out-gunned, and out-manned. Which is what I find surprising about our support for the legal system; we imagine it *serves* and *protects* us. There is overwhelming evidence that it serves and protects those who it is clearly serving and protecting. Did you feel served and protected when you paid a speeding ticket? Imagine an entire city full of people who wanted to use a plant for their own enjoyment (marijuana), and now they are rotting in prisons; were they served and protected?

Individuals run a ponzi scheme—defrauding investors—and go to jail. The government runs a ponzi scheme—social security (yes, it now runs like a ponzi scheme)—and is *legally* allowed to defraud the entire populace. The person who kills a police officer in self-defense goes to jail, often for life. A police officer who executes a harmless citizen on the street in broad daylight is (sometimes) pressured into resigning, (Ian Birk). The government can write something into law in one instance, and then write something else in another (or ignore it altogether).

It's funny that we have various heroes who fought against corrupt laws, yet we never draw the connection that we constantly, actively support the people who prop up an entire system of corrupt laws. Minorities never seem to draw the conclusion that by supporting the government, they support the very laws that have harmed them. We don't revile those who made the corrupt laws to the same degree that we revere the man or woman willing to stand up for a principle. Nor do we ever question that maybe our entire legal system is farcical. The civil rights movement wouldn't have been necessary if slave laws hadn't been written and enforced since the inception of the country. We can all agree that slave laws are unjust (though we continue to allow racist laws on the books in the present), yet that somehow never leads to the questioning of law, of the *legal system,* itself. Somehow, everyone is conditioned to remain faithful—to have faith—in the legal system that was corrupt from it's inception.

But, you better obey the laws while you support one of two law-creating parties currently in power. You disobey laws at your own peril. The rulers haven't just written down words on paper that you have to follow, they've written down more words on paper which tell them— and their minions—how to handle everyone who doesn't dutifully follow. They've created billion dollar agencies of violence to deal with lawbreakers. Central Intelligence Agency. Department of Homeland Security. National Security Agency. Secret Service. Department of Justice (Federal Bureau of Investigation, Bureau of Prisons, Bureau of Alcohol, Tobacco, Firearms, and Explosives, Drug Enforcement Administration). City, county, and state police officers and SWAT teams. The Army, Navy, Air Force, Marines, Coast Guard, and last (but not least, and certainly not a comprehensive list) the National Guard. This isn't your grandmothers wooden spoon.

They'll have your subservience or your life. They'll command the language and twist your emotions to make you feel good about it. They'll design an entire system around hiding the fact from plain view. But at the end of the day—whether you feel good about it or not—it's your obedience or your life.

Laws, especially in current times, are not based on any sort of principle. The entire legal system is not based on any principle of Justice or Freedom. Under what kind of logic is it right for a government to force it's citizens to spend money at particular private businesses (insurance)? Yet this is the pony-show happening now with the new health care laws ruled on by the Supreme Court. Of course, we can argue all kinds of legal theory, philosophy, precedent, and whatnot, imagining that it takes some sort of magic ruling from the divine arbiter of justice in the sky. If only Justice would drop down her holy ruling. Or you can take out the sword of critical thinking and simple logic, cut through all the nonsense, and realize that the health care law, most of our other laws, and even our legal system is superfluous, coercive, and evil.

LAND MONOPOLY

Jean-Jacques Rousseau saw the land monopoly in the year 1754 and wrote:

> "The first man who, having fenced in a piece of land, said "This is mine," and found people naive enough to believe him, that man was the true founder of civil society. From how many crimes, wars, and murders, from how many horrors and misfortunes might not any one have saved mankind, by pulling up the stakes, or filling up the ditch, and crying to his fellows: Beware of listening to this impostor; you are undone if you once forget that the fruits of the earth belong to us all, and the earth itself to nobody."

How can a man, being born into the world free and equal as all men and women, draw out a square on a map and then have the "legal rights" (societally sanctioned violence) to deny any and all access to the land? One man should never be able to own lands with only paper deeds, to the exclusion of society, any more than any government should be able to own lands deeds to the exclusion of all. Land (paper) "ownership" is almost as vile as human ownership (slavery) and leads directly to it.

Morally, how can a life be separated, by violence, from nature; the ability to provide sustenance? If we have a right to life, then we have a right to the means to support life; land. Life without access to land is death or slavery. The current system of land monopolization is a plague of slavery on us all.

If you were granted the freedom to have your own place on the planet, you'd no longer need to pay rent to your landlords. Land, our birthright, is Freedom. All other monopolies exist to deny us the right to land; our birthright.

Land is the ultimate value since it is directly tied to our survival. The accumulation of land is the ultimate wealth. Mistakenly, money is viewed as wealth, since it's a medium of value exchange, but the real value is in land. Back to our basic necessities, food, water, shelter, and clothes; all can be attained with land. If a person or family had access to land, they could theoretically provide for themselves (or barter surplus) indefinitely. Don't take my word for it, look at all of the wealthiest people on the planet. They are *all* very significant landowners.

I want to make sure I am clear. I am not making the point that everyone should live directly off of the land; becoming self-sufficient pioneers. I am making the point that *without access to land, people will always be slaves.* We have been forced off of the land by people who run the law (and their friends) with guns.

A single force having a monopoly on land will always, eventually lead to the enslavement of the population. There is no other alternative, since a life is forcibly removed from the necessities required to sustain it. All we work for today, we work for because we are unable to provide them for ourselves. Problems of homelessness, poverty, foreclosure, hunger, starvation, and bankruptcy are all directly related to land, and the inability to have access.

You have to make a surplus of money at your job(s) because you have to keep paying for all the food, shelter, clothing, and water that you cannot provide yourself. Additionally, you'll require more surplus for your transportation, which isn't a necessity in-and-of itself, but becomes one by virtue of working a job (not located where you sleep) that pays for your other necessities.

As anyone who is poor knows, most of their money is taken up paying rent, food, clothing, and transportation. Even if you should "own" land in the current system, you're still subjected to so many taxes that your work (beyond your own sustenance) may never be finished. Your masters will always require your tribute because you are never fully an owner.

I just spoke to a woman the other day, who "owns" her house on a tiny piece of land two miles away from the city center of Seattle. She pays almost $10,000 a year in property taxes. The poverty threshold for a single person in 2012 (according to HHS) is $11,170. If she was existing at the poverty threshold, her cost of living is almost doubled by virtue of "owning" property. Even if she just sat in her house, everything paid off, and provided all of her own food and water; she would eventually get kicked out of her own house by the landlords without a surplus of money.

Access to land can make a person free. With land, we can provide all of our own necessities and then engage society *voluntarily*. However, if we can never become owners, we are forced to go out and work.

The concept of a free, independent human is revolting to a slave master (and others who lust to control people). Who would feed them? Who would build their houses? Who would valet their Ferraris? Who will fill their banks?

Owners want people to grovel before them. Masters believe themselves better than everyone. Masters maintain control over everyone by controlling the land. Rather, our acquiescence of the system allows them to control the land. All you have to do is study the history of our country to see the truth. The first half our history is riddled with land struggles. More recent American history has been marked by rampant foreign aggression opening foreign markets to United States trade/exploitation; more land, more resources. The world is becoming one giant plantation.

Natural rights are universal and self-evident. Are any born less human than others? How can one human have the natural right to own another from their birth? Only under fictitious claims and the rationale of twisted language can a preposterous case be made. Slavery is impossible under the standing of Natural Law.

We all enter life with an equal claim to our own lives, yet a few on the top are controlling the means to life for all of humanity. One man has unlimited access to land, which is life, and another must grovel at his feet for the hope of being able to use it. Land monopolization is the root of all slavery we can control since all people of the earth must have access to land, or at least the fruits of it, for sustenance. Failure to develop a better system isn't a failure of possibilities, it's a failure of our imagination and willpower. It's a testament to the success of the system in creating generations of brainwashed drones.

No person can be born free into the world to find their own way. Each human must play the government's game of slavery or face destruction. We must play because we cannot live without playing; there is no habitable land that is not owned by the land monopoly. You cannot get food outside of owning land or using the system controlling land. People are destined to spend the rest of their lives chasing the fiction of "ownership"; the land title. Even owning the land is no respite, every state in the Union has property taxes. It's not enough to play the game and carve out a space for yourself, you must continue to slave away to pay your rent to your landlords.

Currently, it is possible to "own" land. If you call being told what to do on your land and paying rent to your masters, "owning". Some land "zoned" for commercial purposes cannot be lived on. Some land “zoned” for residential purposes cannot have a business. You can't build what you want on *your* land; drones enforcing “building codes” will see to that. If you have an HOA, they'll further restrict you on the land you “own”. You're no owner! You're a tenant! They've changed the definition of ownership!

(A quick tangent) It should also be mentioned that a monopoly on agriculture (or a legally supported cartel) is a direct extension of a monopoly on land. When bigmoneyed chemical companies take over agriculture, soon you're eating unpronounceable crap squirted out of a can. Thankfully, bigmoneyed pharmaceutical companies have engineered advanced “drugs” to cure the ill effects of ingesting poisonous food. The government “regulators” who watch over these industries (after having worked in these industries, or made good friends in these industries) make sure that the drugs contain only minor side effects, such as serious injury or death. One day we will discover that a return to more organic, local eating (you know, a healthy lifestyle?) will do far more to reduce horrible illnesses like cancer than wasting your time walking a half marathon to give a donation to the pharmaceutical companies.

It's important to understand: it is really really really difficult to make money off of healthy people who grow their own food (or eat local food). It is much much much easier to make money by making people sick, getting doctors to make them sicker, and then get donations from the same people begging for a cure. I'm sure it's nothing personal... it just makes good business sense. Get 'em coming, get 'em going, and then get a donation on the way out. Sweet deal. (End tangent)

The land monopoly is enforced through law, financed with taxes, both of which are enforced by violence. In a global world of advanced technology, there is nowhere to run; nowhere to begin anew. Only through playing the land game, acquiring a "title", and becoming self-sufficient can a person hope to live as free as possible and engage the world as they wish.

We chase the land because we have to. If not land, then we have to chase money. Once you chase the money, once you give up the prospect of self-reliance, they've got you forever. You'll need to keep working until you die or, God forbid, retire. They'll steal from you as you're retired, steal from you should you try to invest any of your money, and then try to steal what you might attempt to pass to a relative. Those who chase the money are certain to never escape the gerbil wheel. This is the basis of investment theories such as Robert Kiyosaki's *Rich Dad Poor Dad;* take charge of your own investments and get other people to pay you rent. It's an unending game of thievery and enslavement. Play or die.

A.J. Ogilvy demonstrated the transition from (what we used to call) slavery to (what still is) slavery in "A Colonists Plea for Land Nationalization"—written around 1890 in Australia:

> Suppose I own a sugar estate and 100 slaves, all the land about being held in the same way by people of the same class as myself. It is a profitable business, but there are many expenses and annoyances attached to it.
>
> I must keep up my supply of slaves either by breeding or buying them. I must pay an overseer to keep them continually to their work with the lash. I must keep them in a state of brutish ignorance (to the detriment of their efficiency), for fear they should learn their rights and their power, and become dangerous. I must tend them in sickness and when past work.

And the slaves have all the vices and defects that slavery engenders; they have no self-respect or moral sense; they lie, they steal, they are lazy, shirking work whenever they dare; they do not care what mischief their carelessness occasions me so long as it is not found out; their labour is obtained by force, and given grudgingly; they have no heart in it.

All these things worry me.

Suddenly a brilliant idea strikes me. I reflect that there is no unoccupied land in the neighbourhood, so that if my labourers were free they would still have to look to me for work somehow.

So one day I announce to them that they are all free, intimating at the same time that I will be ready to employ as many as I may require on such terms as we may mutually and independently agree.

What could be fairer? They are overjoyed, and falling on their knees, bless me as their benefactor. They then go away and have a jollification, and next day come back to me to arrange the new terms. Most of them think they would like to have a piece of land and work it for themselves, and be their own masters. All they want is the few tools they have been accustomed to use, and some seed, and these they are ready to buy from me, undertaking to pay me with reasonable interest when the first crop comes in, offering the crop as security. As for their keep they can easily earn that by working a few weeks on and off any of the plantations, or by taking a job of clearing, fencing, or such like. This will keep them going for the first year, and after that they will be better able to take care of themselves.

"But" softly, I observe, "you are going too fast. Your proposals about the tools and seed and your maintenance are all right enough, but the land, you must remember, belongs to me. You cannot expect me to give you your own liberty and my land too for nothing. That would not be reasonable, would it?" They agree that it would not, and begin to propose terms.

A fancies this bit of land and *B* that. But it soon appears that I want this bit of land for my next year's clearing, and that for my cows, and another is too close to my house, and would interfere with my privacy, and another is thick forests or swamp, and would require too long and costly preparation for men who must have quick returns in order to live, and in short that there is no land suitable that I care to part with.

Still I am ready to do what I promised "to employ as many as I may require, on such terms as we may mutually and independently agree to." But as I have now to pay them wages instead of getting their work for nothing, I cannot of course employ quite so many of them. I can find work for ninety of them, however, and with these I am prepared to discuss terms.

At once a number volunteer their services at such wages as their imagination has been picturing to them. I tell the ninety whose demands are most reasonable, to stand on one side. The remaining ten look blank, and seeing that since I won't let them have any of the land, it is a question of hired employment or starvation, they offer to come for a little less than the others. I tell these now to stand aside, and ten others to stand out instead. These look blank now, and offer to work for less still, and so the "mutual and voluntary" settlement of terms proceeds.

But, meanwhile, I have been making a little calculation in my head, and have reckoned up what the cost of keeping a slave, with his food and clothes, and a trifle over to keep him contented, would come to, and I offer that

They won't hear of it, but as I know they can't help themselves, I say nothing, and presently first one and then another gives in, till I have got my ninety, and still there are ten left out, and very blank indeed they look. Whereupon, the terms being settled, I graciously announce that though I don't really want any more men, still I am willing (in my benevolence) to take the ten, too, on the same terms, which they promptly accept, and again hail me as their benefactor, only not quite so rapturously as before.

So they all set to at the old work at the old place, and on the old terms, only a little differently administered; that is, that whereas I formerly supplied them with food, clothes, etc., direct from my stores, I now give them a weekly wage representing the value of those articles, which they will henceforth have to buy for themselves.

There is a difference too in some other respects, indicating a moral improvement in our relations. I can no longer curse and flog them. But then I don't want to; it's no longer necessary; the threat of dismissal is quite as effective, even more so; and much pleasanter for me. I can no longer separate husband from wife, parent from child. But then again, I don't want to. There would be no profit in it; leaving them their wives and children has the double advantage of making them more contented with their lot, and giving me greater power over them, for they have now got to keep these wives and children out of their own earnings.

My men are now as eager to come to me to work as they formerly were to run away from work.
I have neither to buy nor to breed them; and if any suddenly leave me, instead of letting loose the bloodhounds, I have merely to hold up a finger or advertise, and I have plenty of others offering in their place.

I am saved the expense and worry of incessant watching and driving. I have no sick to tend, or worn-out pensioners to maintain. If a man falls ill, there is nothing but my good nature to prevent my turning him off at once; the whole affair is a purely commercial transaction; so much wages for so much work. The patriarchal relation of slave-owner and slave is gone, and no other has taken its place.

When the man is worn out with long service, I can turn him out with a clear business conscience, knowing that the State will see that he does not starve. Instead of being forced to keep my men in brutish ignorance, I find public schools established at other people's expense to stimulate their intelligence and improve their minds, to my great advantage, and their children compelled to attend these schools. The service I get, too, being now voluntarily rendered (or apparently so) is much improved in quality.

In short, the arrangement pays me better in every way.

But I gain in other ways besides pecuniary profit. I have lost the stigma of being a slave driver, and have acquired instead the character of a man of energy and enterprise, of justice and benevolence. I am a "large employer of labour," to whom the whole country, and the labourer especially, is greatly indebted. The people say, "See the power of capital! These poor labourers, having no capital, could not use the land if they had it, so this great and far-seeing man wisely refuses to let them have it, and keeps it all himself, but, by providing them with employment, his capital saves them from pauperism, and enables him to build up the wealth of the country, and his own fortune together."

Whereas it is not my capital that does any of these things. It is not my capital but the labourer's toil that builds up my fortune and the wealth of the country. My capital at the most only puts a few better instruments into his hands than he could procure for himself.

It is not my employment that keeps him from pauperism, but my monopoly of the land forcing him into my employment that keeps him on the brink of it. It is not want of capital that prevents the labourer from using the land, but my refusing him the use of the land that prevents him from acquiring capital. All the capital he wants (to begin with) is an axe and a spade, which a week's earnings would buy him; and for his maintenance during the first year, and at any subsequent time, he could work for me or for others, turn about, with his work on his own land. Henceforth with every year, his capital would grow of itself, and his independence with it; and that this is no fancy sketch, anyone can see for himself by taking a trip to our NorthWest Coast, (Tasmania) where he will find well-to-do farmers who began with nothing but a spade and an axe (so to speak) and worked their way up in the manner described.

But now another thought strikes me. Instead of paying an overseer to work these men for me, I will make him pay me for the privilege of doing it. I will let the land as it stands to him or to another, to whomsoever will give the most for the billet. He shall be called my tenant instead of my overseer, but the thing he shall do for me is essentially the same, only done by contract instead of for yearly pay.

He, not I, shall find all the capital, take all the risk, and engage and supervise the men, paying me a lump sum, called rent, out of the proceeds of their toil, and make what he can for himself out of the surplus. The competition is as keen in its way for the land, among people of his class, as it is among the labourers for employment, only that as they are all possessed of some little means (else they could not compete) they are in no danger of immediate want and can stand out for rather better terms than the labourers who are forced by necessity to take what terms they can get.

The minimum in each case amounts practically to a "mere living," but the mere living they insist on is one of a rather higher standard, than the labourer's; it means a rather more abundant supply, and better quality of those little comforts which are next door to necessaries. It means, in short, a living of the kind to which people of that class are accustomed.

For a moderate reduction in my profits then (a reduction equal to the tenant's narrow margin of profit) I have all the toil and worry of management taken off my hands and the risk too, for, be the season good or bad, the rent is bound to be forthcoming, and I can sell him up to the last rag if he fails of the full amount, no matter for what reason, and my rent takes precedence of all other debts.

All my capital is set free for investment elsewhere, and I am freed from the odium of a slaveowner,

> notwithstanding that the men still toil for my enrichment as when they were my slaves, and that I get more out of them than ever.
>
> If I wax rich while they toil from hand to mouth, and in depressed seasons find it hard to get work at all; it is not, to all appearance, my doing, but merely the force of circumstances, the law of nature, the state of the labour market; fine-sounding names that hide the ugly reality.
>
> If wages are forced down, it is not I who do it, it is that greedy and merciless man, the employer (my tenant) who does it. I am a lofty and superior being, dwelling apart and above such sordid circumstances. I would never dream of grinding these poor labourers, not I! I have nothing to do with them at all, I only want my rent and get it. Like the lilies of the field I toil not, neither do I spin, and yet (so kind is Providence!) my daily bread (well-buttered) comes to me of itself. Nay, people bid against each other for the privilege of finding it for me; and no one seems to realise that the comfortable income that falls to me like the refreshing dew is dew indeed, but it is the dew of sweat wrung from the labourer's toil. It is the fruit of their labour which they ought to have; which they would have if I did not take it from them.
>
> Is this caricature?

———

It should still be possible to own land. However, ownership is not conferred with a document any more than education is. Ownership is mastery. The one who masters the land is the owner. Death ends ownership so that another may become an owner; a master. The true concept of ownership is obvious; only the one who can use it (or is using it) is the one who can own it.

Ownership, conferred by mastery, wouldn't allow for eminent domain and public road building. This would drastically slow down the speed of businesses/

governments paving everything. They would encounter real landowners every step of the way. We've got a legion of corporations who are landowners now; will an individual ever have access to that land again? We're cordoning off cemeteries and blocking out "historical sites" that the living will never be able to use again. Who's Earth is this? It must belong to a select group of governments, their friends, corporations, historical sites, and dead people; if we look at who "owns" the land. Homeless people roaming the streets and millions scraping up the rent? No problem here! That's how the system is designed!

The owner should be the one who has dominion. The one who cultivates the land, lives in harmony with the land, sustains him/herself off of the land, should be the owner of it. In the case of Ted Turner (who owns land equivalent to three times Rhode Island), I can't imagine anyone owns most of his land. Any land going unused has no real owner. Much of our land in this country goes unused, by design, and remains vacant; unowned. This land is purposefully set aside so that you and I will fight each other for the leftovers. Imagine what would happen to property value if all land was opened up to be used by everyone. In fact, the very concept of "property value" is stupid; what's the real price of life? Life without land is death, or slavery. Slave masters can't have people sustaining themselves on their own land. A dairy farm isn't run with wild cows indiscriminately roaming the countryside.

This is not a call to bulldoze the earth. If we experienced a closer tie to our natural environment, we would be the protectors and cultivators of it. If each man had to acquire some of his own sustenance from the land (or—at the very least—understood his relationship with it), he would be a lot more hesitant to poison or destroy it; to poison the land would be to poison himself. The current state of the division of labor means that most people do not understand their relationship to the environment. What does the trader on Wall St. understand about what nature provides for him?

This is not an idea for world peace. There will always be evil people and deadly force will always need to be met with deadly force. It is an idea for *much less* violence and coercion. How can we have equality in a world of kings and peasants? It's true that the rulers understand our plight; they've put up the fences around us!

This is a call to end slavery! We need to bring an end to the monopolization of land! Why should a few men control (by force) the sustenance of all of humanity? Millions starve to death or work endlessly because a few people have put a fence around our birthright and recruit a few stooges to shoot any *trespassers.* Millions fall for it because their minds have been deformed by linguistic and emotional manipulation. Millions can't figure it out because the scheme has been diversified in many layers.

Only when people are free to make their own way in the world, which begins with using the land for their necessities, can we have a chance at living with less violence! Until then, poverty, starvation, violence, slavery, thievery, extortion, and murder will be the rule, not the exception. Do you want to stop poverty, starvation, slavery, thievery, extortion, and murder? Do you want to have a hope at living in a less violent world? Do you aspire to live peacefully amongst peaceful neighbors? Then you have to stop supporting the system that keeps setting the table for poverty, starvation, violence, thievery, destruction, and death.

Those with access to land will always live easy, on the backs of slaves. Those without will struggle until death.

"Land monopoly is not the only monopoly, but it is by far the greatest of monopolies -- it is a perpetual monopoly, and it is the mother of all other forms of monopoly." -Winston Churchill

A QUESTION NEVER ASKED

Wealth is an accumulation of value. Value is created over time as resources are created or become more useful. For example, we could go out into the woods and chop a tree into lumber. We've created value; added the value of the lumber to the total economy. We could take the lumber and use it to build a house. Now we've added the value of a house to the economy (minus the value of available lumber). In a business flipping houses, no value is added to the economy. Nothing was created or made more useful.

Technology is largely responsible for the increase of wealth in modern times. Technology allows a person to control more resources than they could before. Rather than haul goods in a horse drawn wagon, we can drive them in a semi-truck. It used to take a team of men a particular time to dig a massive hole. Now one man with a backhoe can complete the task in a fraction of the time. Workers on a building site used to hammer nails. Now the nail gun allows the worker to build the project in a fraction of the time. Essentially, technology allows a person to perform more than they were able to perform previously; control more resources. As technology has increased, our wealth has increased; our ability to generate wealth has increased.

Wealth also increases over time. I can chop lumber for one day and I'll have one day's-worth of value. After one year of chopping, I'd have a year's-worth of value. Over time, I create additional value. Labor, multiplied by technology, over time, creates wealth.

Here's the question. Roughly a hundred years ago, the eight hour work day became standard in the United States. In the last one hundred years, there has been a host of technological advances that have made labor more productive and allowed us to generate more wealth than ever before. We have also had the benefit of one hundred years of wealth generation. If that is true, why are people still working eight hours a day, or more?

Wouldn't technological breakthroughs facilitate the creation of exponentially more wealth, allowing people to work much less to meet basic necessities? Where is all the wealth going? Considering a host of technological breakthroughs and (what should have been) the accumulation of wealth, we should be working a fraction of the time people worked a hundred years ago. Where has all the wealth gone?

Some of our loss is because our greed has outpaced our needs. Americans are ever greater consumers. Some of our wealth has also left the country. The wealth that goes with production has fled with our ability to produce.

Aside from those, a large part of our loss is through wealth funneling upward to the masters and overseers. Through the litany of taxes, cartels and monopolies have been taking the wealth as fast as technology can increase our production. Massive social programs. Huge government bureaucracy. Simultaneous wars. Cartelized industries. If time is our most valuable resource, a hundred years of labor and technology has left us negligibly better than our ancestors, thanks to the middlemen. Our grandparents labored eight hours a day to survive and the inheritance we have been left has amounted to, quite literally, nothing.

A wealthier lifestyle isn't more debt. Record levels of consumer debt, mortgages, and student loans isn't an indication of wealth.

So where has all the wealth from the last 100 years gone??

PRIVATIZATION/PUBLICIZATION

Our system of society presently operates for the benefit of a few—to the detriment of all others—through the privatization of profits and publicization of losses. This takes shape through centralization of government and business. Laws are made in support of bigger businesses and government parties, guaranteeing further profits. These laws are upheld by law enforcement, paid for by the general public through taxation (the first subsidy).

As an example, taxes taken to spend on roads only benefit people who use the roads. Taxes spent on specific purposes only help those who benefit from the specific purpose. The ones who take best personal advantage of the laws (oftentimes the ones making them, or their friends) are the real beneficiaries. A few people make astonishing profits within the system, paid for by the general public.

A second, more obvious subsidy (or publicization) is when the government or central banks get involved in literal subsidies of governments and businesses; handing them cash (such as Solyndra). The cash has to come from somewhere. It comes from taxpayers. The businesses take the money and reap the profits for themselves. (Sometimes, in the case of a loan, they pay it back, which raises the question as to why select businesses should benefit from government favors.)

The Federal Reserve and the government have done this time and again. Losses come at the expense of the tax slave, while profits go directly to the company or individuals; CEO's, bankers, who, in turn, make large campaign contributions or energize a voter base (perpetuate an illusion). It's a sick cycle of funneling money upward and keeping it there. It's a system—

ultimately a way in which most Americans have been conned into thinking—which is designed to funnel wealth upward; to impoverish and enslave the citizenry while a few get wealthy off the folks who labor.

The solution to these shenanigans isn't more laws requiring the redistribution of money in a downward direction. The solution is that we need to quit the legal sanction of the government and the private bank of the Federal Reserve to keep subsidizing a few businesses, foreign countries, and each other, with taxpayer money; a few people riding high at the expense of 'the public'.

When economies are destroyed, it's not the people with billions of dollars who are hurting; oftentimes they've *caused* them to tank. When interest rates and inflation go up, it's not the people with hundreds of millions of dollars who are hurting. When taxes get increased, it's not the people with tens of millions of dollars who are struggling to eat. The poorer you are, the more easily you are abused by the current system. Yet, the poorest people in society are often the most fervent supporters of the system itself. A system that drains their lives so a few on top can live comfortably. A privatization of profits. A publicization of losses. A system of slavery dependent on the slaves for maintenance.

THE GREATEST COMMON DIVISOR AND PROBLEMS OF SCALE

The greatest common divisor—typically expressed as the "least common denominator"—is essentially a mathematical understanding of compromise. Society as a whole does not yet appreciate the truth of it.

Imagine you're working on a project. Whatever solution you can come up with for the project is only limited by your abilities and your standards of excellence. Now imagine its a two-person project. The project will only attain as much excellence as the two of you can agree on and implement. Now imagine a project with one hundred people. How can you accommodate the standards of excellence of one hundred people? Any compromise will have to be so base as to be acceptable and useful to one hundred people. Now imagine a million...

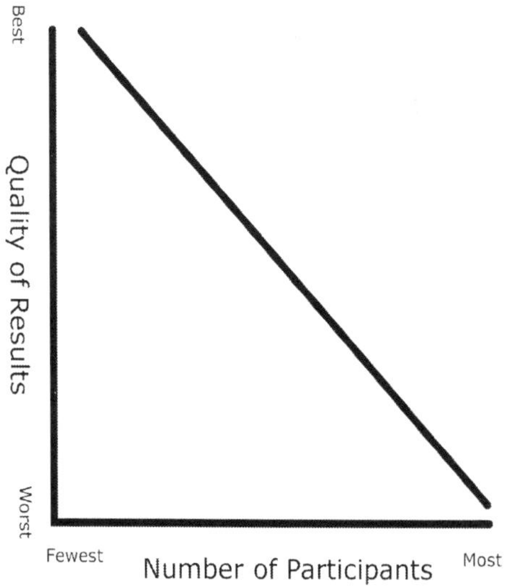

The concept should be obvious. Small targeted charities are often very effective but not very broad reaching. Broad reaching measures such as welfare are all encompassing and almost entirely ineffectual. The larger the area of compromise, the lower (worse/less effective) the compromise becomes.

Entertainment is ample evidence. Wildly popular movies, music, and books achieve success in one of two ways. Occasionally, a work of art strikes a cord across the emotions and imaginations of the masses. However, popular works are typically so basic as to have a slight appeal across a large spectrum. (Hence, the creation of "market research") The focused movie about a tough subject, the music with thoughtful lyrics, or the book that makes you think, will often lose out (in popularity) over the mindless summer blockbuster, catchy pop song about partying on the roof, or quick thriller book (DaVinci Code holds a special place in my heart as one of the worst books I have ever read). It's easy for a hundred million people to zone out to explosions on a movie screen for two hours. It's harder for a hundred million people to appreciate the complexity of characters working through difficulty in life.

Society continually attempts to centralize and enlarge, despite clear natural evidence that this is the road to horrible results.

Socialism (pooling together resources, singular authority, and sharing) might work brilliantly with five people, or fifty, but it doesn't work so hot with 100 million. The wants, desires, and needs of five people are measurable and easily comprehended. It is much easier to find common ground with five people than 100 million. When you have one person (the "public servant", central planner) making decisions for the group, it's much easier to make decisions for five people than 100 million people.

Democracy works brilliantly with two people but suffers a serious drop off with the increase to three. In a three person democracy, two people can bully around the third every time. The truth of democracy is, "two wolves and a sheep deciding what's for lunch." It gets worse as the population gets larger. Soon you've got 50.1 million people eating 49.9 million people for lunch; a recipe for unhappiness, disaster, and death.

Aside from the majority always bullying the minority, the problem of scale—the drop-off in quality—is one reason why democracy gets worse as populations increase. Any solution good enough to accommodate one million people is almost guaranteed to be ineffectual, at best, and certainly worse than a solution for thousands, or hundreds. As scale increases, not only do problems increase, but problems *from* scale begin to appear.

"Too big to fail" is foolish slogan of the times. Oftentimes the reason a giant organization or government fails is *because* it has gotten too big in the first place! Since largess of scale is often the cause of many problems, there can be no such thing as "too big to fail". As scale increases, problems increase. As problems increase, the likelihood of disaster increases in kind.

Largess—excess scale—in-and-of itself is a recipe for disaster. As scale increases, quality-of-results are guaranteed to drop off. Empires and large companies assume they can defy the rule. The shattering of empires and large countries throughout history, and utterly low quality of the goods and services of large companies, all attest to inescapable problems of scale. As our country grows in power and wealth, destruction *because* of our largess is almost assured. Sadly, the ones who are crushed under the collapse aren't the same ones who benefited from the ascension. The ones who built the tower with their labors are the ones who are crushed.

HYPOCRISY

In an honest world, all unprincipled political opinions will be prefaced with the phrase, “When I am dictator...”

Everyone who rejects violence being used against them and then advocates forcing other people to live as they do is simply a hypocrite.

Proponents of violence must choose to change—to live non-violently—or they themselves will have to be violently resisted.

But violence—death and destruction—is the antithesis of peace, prosperity, wealth, and happiness; we cannot have both.

A MONOPOLY OF VIOLENCE

Winston Churchill, whom I quoted in the chapter on land, was wrong. Land isn't the greatest monopoly; violence is. A lot of land—and very few guns—can't last forever, as the indigenous people of America unfortunately discovered.

Violence is the greatest monopoly. The ability to kill ends the discussion; death is an abrupt period. There is no negotiation when one party has a gun and the other is unarmed, or when one party has nuclear weapons and the other has rifles. There is only theft, rape, and murder. Violence is the ultimate monopoly because it enforces all other monopolies; there is no other monopoly without a monopoly on violence. Competition can arise against any monopoly in a free environment, but none can arise in the face of death and destruction. Violence—theft and murder—is all that is needed to enforce slavery.

However, it's not just violence, or the threat of violence. It's a superior amount of force; a monopoly on violence. Countries with nuclear weapons aren't attacking each other, for obvious reasons. Just like we don't see any people shooting up random crowds of people in Montana or Texas. An armed peaceful party is deterrence. Thieves and murderers aren't stupid, initiating violence against another party where the consequences are likely to be injury or death aren't worth it. It's not enough to have the capacity for violence; it must be a much higher capacity, or a monopoly.

The picture paints itself. Each person is responsible for their own capacity for defense. Each community is responsible for itself. Each country. In a world where evil people exist, only a fool argues for disarmament (nuclear weapons are a little trickier, in this respect). A world where everyone has a gun is perceived as being dangerous, but a disarmed world has *proven* to be dangerous. I would question the sanity of anyone who would argue that upwards of a million Hutus died in Rwanda because they were too well armed. Any individual who gives up the right to defend himself—willingly or not—becomes a ripe target. Slaves (and victims) throughout history, the world over, have been made of people who were unable to defend themselves against superiorly armed evil people.

The logical fallacies are hopefully obvious at this point. The initiation of violence is evil. Claiming to own land is farcical. Writing down the ability to steal or murder doesn't create a moral justification. Except, this is how we run our society. A claim to land is assumed. A right to violence is supposedly granted, and just. A monopoly on law is the natural succession from monopolies of land and violence. Slaves can never truly own anything. Slaves are not allowed to defend themselves.

A trite argument I'd like to nip in the bud is, "But we can defend ourselves. We're allowed to purchase guns." Yes, you can defend yourself...from other citizens. Try defending yourself from the law or try defending yourself from the taxman when he comes around for his portion of your earnings. There is no defense from the government. They can arrest you anytime they like, throw you in jail for anything they like, or kill you just as well if that suffices. The only trick is that they can't do too much of this, they have to keep up the *illusion* that the diary farm is safe, otherwise the cows might get spooked. Frightened, angry cows are bad for dairy production.

If you can separate a life from it's means of living, you have created a slave. If you want to run a plantation successfully, and much more productively, you own the slave's mind. The willing slave is a thousand times more productive than the one who is beaten into submission. But, a fence and a gun are the only requirements to run a plantation.

History is written by the victors. The last one living gets the last word. And so the history that we revere—most of the history we read, the history that shapes our view of the world—was written, not by the most enlightened society, the greatest humanitarians, or the most advanced cultures, but by the people who perfected the use of violence in their times. From the phalanx's of Greece to the atomic bomb, history is a narrative of the nations who achieved the greatest success in obliterating other nations. Of course, those people who were destroyed were uncultured, uncivilized brutes; lives wasted in the mud anyhow, right? At least, according to historical record.

We understand that history is written by the victors, but we haven't understood how history has tainted our understanding of victory. History portrays victory as the destruction of one's enemy. History is the triumph of good over evil (unless Nazi Germany had won WW2, in which case history would have been the triumph of....well, good over evil, because then the good guys writing history would have been Nazi's). History is (allegedly) a glorious legacy of noble warriors upholding civilization against the evil people of their day.

History, in that respect, is nothing more than a narrative of violence. If I went to the apartment next door, shot my neighbor, and incorporated everything he owns into my own goods (let's call my "goods" my "empire"), would I be hailed as a man of my time? Civilizing my brutish neighbor who chose to live differently than me, haven't I just created a whole new era of peace and prosperity within my apartment building? We revile the man who murders his neighbors but praise the nations who murder theirs. Is it so different?

Or what if I just knocked on every door in my apartment complex and told them that we had new rules for the complex. Everyone can do whatever they like, so long as I approve it, because it's the law (rules I wrote down on some paper). I own the building now (I bought it out, killed the owner, doesn't matter) and I am going to be enforcing the law with my gun. Even better, I'll get a friend or two with guns to patrol the complex and make sure everyone is obeying. Everyone has to do as the law says (I write the law, with the help of my friends, aka the "representatives") or else we'll rip them out of their apartment and lock them in my empty closet (or kill them). Would you want to live in this apartment complex? Is this the paragon of civilized society? Is this the best way for people to live amongst each other?

Then we decide that the neighboring apartment complex is brutish and uncivilized (or that they have a lot of stuff that we'd like for ourselves). I'll get my tenants fired up about how great our apartment complex is. Complex of the free. Complex of the brave. And then we'll go subjugate the other complex into our empire, or kill them. Whatever, just so long as we get some of their stuff. We're doing them a favor, really, opening up their apartment complex to trade and democracy; civilization. One building leads to another. We'll even let the tenants choose who they want to be the leader, from pre-approved choices. Who says tenants can't choose their own fate? Soon we'll bring peace, prosperity, and democracy to the whole neighborhood.

If this really happened in your neighborhood, would you imagine these are civilized, peaceful people? How much mental and emotional manipulation has to take place for these people to be considered noble purveyors of peace and prosperity? The tenants who are subjugated at the point of a gun will know better, but their children or great grandchildren will eventually be persuaded differently.

And somehow we all agree that this is the best way to live together in society. One group of people should be able to run everything at the point of a gun. Anyone who disagrees, regardless of whether they are peaceful and productive on their own, is jailed or killed.

Violence is the best way to have a non-violent, peaceful, prosperous society? We're not capable of working out differences with our neighbors? We're not capable of coming together voluntarily to solve problems?

It has been said that war is merely politics by other means and politics is merely economics by other means. Essentially, war replaces exchange. This is the fundamental misunderstanding in all of the political rhetoric about free markets. If governments understood the concepts and benefits of free markets, they would abolish themselves (and if people understood the nature of governments they would have abolished them themselves long before governments could come to this realization). There is no trading with governments; there is no peaceful exchange with violence.

Instead we view victory as the slaughter of our enemies, instead of talking with them, reaching understanding with them, exchanging freely with them, and becoming mutually prosperous together. The goal of nations is victory, not peace and prosperity. If that weren't the case, wouldn't we have increasingly less enemies and wars? When people meet each other as equals, there can be trade and prosperity. When one is threatened with injury or death, there is only robbery, slavery, and murder.

So life is reduced to a petty struggle to become the boss of the apartment complex; dominate or kill your neighbors, lest you be dominated and killed yourself. History, with few exceptions, is merely a record of the most successful gangsters; thugs. Civilizations that have risen to the top haven't done so because of freedom, prosperity, or whatever other concept they have been ennobled with after the fact, ours included. Civilizations that have risen to the top have done so because their bosses best succeeded at the use of violence; against other peoples, and against their own.

PERPETUAL MOTION

Slavery doesn't perpetuate itself. On a planet of humans —clearly born as free individuals—it must be instituted and consciously pursued.

> "To make a contented slave it is necessary to make a thoughtless one. It is necessary to darken the moral and mental vision and, as far as possible, to annihilate the power of reason." -Frederick Douglass

Slavery has proven to be the world's first perpetual motion machine. Slaves, kept in the cycle, will spin for their entire lives; perfect dairy cows. It's a three-part, cycle, continuously flowing into itself; too ignorant to know any better, too busy to pay attention, and too comfortable to resist.

We must be kept busy, comfortable, and ignorant. If we aren't busy, then we'll have time to learn, think, and grow on our own. We have to stay busy so it appears (to ourselves) that we're creating something (remember that "retirement" you're slowly saving up for (after you pay rent)?). We have to stay relatively comfortable; people who have nothing to lose are willing to fight for something better. And we have to stay ignorant; if we realized how were were fleeced and abused every day, we wouldn't stand for it. Everything conceded by those in control is to further maintain the cycle; keep the dairy cows producing. I am not aware of a single instance of power being willingly relinquished, without an ulterior motive discovered later. Small concessions of power—keep the system in tact while maintaining the illusion of freedom—keep the dairy farm running smoothly.

It's difficult to make money during a slave rebellion, as the British learned in 1776, or our previous Presidents learned for the first 150 years of the country. Owners didn't make much money when workers were idle, starved, angry, or self-reliant. Starved, angry workers were striking on company property, fighting the authorities, or off doing their own thing. It's bad business to get into a fistfight with your slaves; money doesn't make itself (Federal Reserve jokes aside). Nobody—including me—wants to see outright violence in society; even the owners don't want to see outright violence, it's bad for business (unless you're waging wars in other countries to open foreign markets).

The system has plenty of functions to induce and support ignorance. School are churning out indecisive drones by the millions. News, media, propaganda, and unending entertainment. One can know everything about the Kardashians and nothing about living.

The infiltration of the mainstream media has been a huge victory for those in power. By only reporting on approved stories, they control the conversation. Love him or hate him, Ron Paul clearly exposed the machinations of the media and the "democracy" of the political parties in his run for president this year. Cursory research into the (lack of) media coverage, stolen delegates, imprisoned and bullied campaign officers, changing rules in the middle of the contest, and non/mis-counting of votes shows how the game is rigged. Elections in Rome were won by the man with the most money and thugs; how is it any different in the United States? The only difference, as far as I can see, is that we attempt to create the illusion that this isn't the case. The collusion of the media with the moneyed slave masters is designed to keep people ignorant, distracted, and believing in an illusion.

> "Americans are made to feel free by the exercise of meaningless choices." -George Carlin

They're busy talking about gay marriage on the news. Try this one on: regardless of the decision, government controls marriage. If the government allows gay marriage, the government controls marriage. If the government does not allow gay marriage, the government controls marriage. Both straight and gay fools will be fighting each other until the end of time, much to the amusement of the slave masters. Nobody bothers to ask why government should have any say in marriage at all? Those in power remain in power. Those making money keep making money. And those in power can stay busy with all kinds of other under-the-table shenanigans while everyone is distracted with (what should be) a complete non-issue; murder around the globe, manipulating other countries, manipulating the currency, consolidating business interests, and robbing citizens.....keep talking about gay marriage, every second wasted on that nonsense is another second the chains are hammered tighter around your ankles!

Should a man overcome ignorance, he's still got to make his way in the world. You've got to eat. You've got to pay those taxes. You've got to pay rent to your landlord; and if you "own" land, pay property taxes to the other landlord. You've got to buy clothes, pay for shelter, and insure it all.

The slave masters make the most money when the dairy cows are happily working. The owners make much less money in times of rebellion. It's in their interest to keep the herd *comfortably busy.* Whether this is human nature or by design, all of society is structured around keeping us too busy to think and too comfortable to resist. It's no coincidence that a majority of the violent uprisings around the world have coincided with extremely high food prices. An idle, hungry populace is not one that is going to be happily milked.

The illusion that we're working for ourselves must be maintained, even if more than half of our earned value is taken away. It has to appear as if we can make progress in our own lives, however slowly, so we'll keep chasing it. As long as it appears as if we can do something for ourselves, we'll keep doing it. Giving up hope (sitting and doing nothing), or fighting back are recipes for a lost investment on the part of the owners. Staying busy hinges on maintaining the illusion and maintaining ignorance; and the cycle continues.

(Unfortunately, the cycle will probably continue until most of the population is completely despoiled, hopelessly in debt, and low on resources... then what?)

Should a man overcome ignorance and necessity, there are innumerable entertainment options to lure him back into ignorance, or apathy. Books, movies, music, television, sports, the Internet, and video games all offer a way to be entertained into oblivion. Many Americans experience a thousand lives without ever living a single one. Many Americans avoid a harsh reality by living in fantasy lands.

Should one or two individuals rise above ignorance and perpetual poverty, no matter. They are easily lulled to sleep. There's enough entertainment to keep them occupied. And at that point, they've got too much to risk on any discomfort anyhow. The dairy farm continues unhampered if one or two cows are able to jump the fence.

Or, should the individual realize an ill in society and attempt to do something about it, there is innumerable problems to work on which will never be solved. The owners don't mind if people give their whole lives to good, charitable causes; the system that causes the ills remains intact.

Homelessness will never go away so long as land is roped off and people are denied access. Yet, we have vast networks of charities struggling to build small structures for the poor and destitute, one-at-a-time. We have a banking system sitting on millions of empty homes, "legally" stolen from consumers on the grounds of "poor choices".

If the solution to homelessness isn't apparent in those two sentences, I don't know what else to say. If I could use my guns to make you use my currency, have my banks pressure you into buying a house, and then blow your currency (pieces of paper) up and take the house.. that's a sweet deal! And I'm not alleging conspiracy here, but if you call the play in plain English, that's what it looks like. The government enforces the laws that allows the Federal Reserve to pump the economy full of money and ensures bad loans, banks are pressured by profit and public to make infinite money therefore hard selling bad loans, people are sold the idea of housing as a safe investment. And once the ponzi scheme reached peak capacity, millions got foreclosed on and banks consolidated their wealth via taxpayer bailout. If you wanted to run a system, this is the way to do it!

Banks are back to making money. The average person is struggling to survive. People are angry at the banks but the banks are the patsies of the Federal Reserve and the thugs called law circling it. Many selflessly labor away in an attempt to help each other while cigar-smoking owners are toasting each other on the rooftop decks of skyscrapers. They tip their hats to you. It's a beautiful game.

The bottom line is simple: *power is never given* up. The cycle of slavery will continue indefinitely so long as people are kept ignorant, busy, and comfortable. Is there an empire that wasn't built on an ignorant, busy, and comfortable population (and mastery of warfare)? Consequently, an ignorant, busy, and comfortable population is crushed underfoot as empires topple inward on themselves, once resources and production have been greedily cannibalized. People in power will only relinquish power to avoid rebellion and revolution. If you're too busy to contemplate your surroundings, no cessation of power is necessary. If you're too comfortable to stand up and say “No!”, no cessation of power is necessary. If you're comfortably entertained into a stupor, no cessation of power is necessary. Historically, things go poorly for slave masters when the slaves get fed up with abuse, get too hungry, have no other outlet, or simply become aware of their situation.

And so long as you do what you're told, you uphold the systems of power that are turning the screws on...you! You support the system at *your* expense. You go to work every day, paying for the privilege of working for the benefit of your owners.

Dairy cows have easygoing, sweet lives until their production becomes unprofitable, or they become unruly. Then they—dried husks of their former selves—are turned out to pasture, left for dead...or worse.

A NEW AGE

"All tyranny needs to gain a foothold is for people of good conscience to remain silent." -Thomas Jefferson

The first question I always get is, "so what's the solution?" I think it's a misleading question. There is no solution. There never will be. In an imperfect world, there will always be imperfections; a downward slippery slope. There will always be evil, to which there is no end and therefore no "solution".

A better question is, "What can I do?" The answer to which could be an entire book on it's own; everything! If the world as we know it is the aggregate of the choices of each person, each man and woman affects the direction of the world, of their country, of their community, and ultimately their own lives *every second.* I've heard it said that, "the first trick of the Devil was to convince people that he didn't exist", and regardless of anyone's religious beliefs, the moral holds. Complacence is all evil needs to run it's course.

The same could be said for good motives, that (behind a powerful leader) they too could flourish in a complacent society, but what kind of good-intentioned person sets out to control other people? The "freedom to do as I say for your own benefit" is just as noble as the freedom to be a slave, or the freedom to be murdered. It is only evil that wishes to dominate others. It is only evil that seeks to rob, kill, and destroy at it's own whim. And evil requires a legion of soldiers to do it's bidding. It doesn't really matter whether the soldier is evil or ignorant; murder is murder.

For example, this is why I do not support any troops who follow immoral orders. Almost all orders given to our troops are immoral; therefore, unsupportable. Or would

Nazi civilians have been justified in "supporting the troops" while opposing Nazism?

The truth is, anyone has the power to do anything. Anyone can be anything. Anyone can do anything. Each of us is blessed with a life that is uniquely our own, and each of us faces a series of choices that is uniquely our own. As I mentioned earlier, I (like many others) would love to just live and let live. However, we are not left to live.

Monopolies intrude into our lives every second of every day. We're tenants on the governments land. We exist as they see fit, at the barrel of their guns. We are restricted to their roads, the food they should see fit for us to eat, the programs they approve for television, and whatever other hoop they should want us to jump through, or else be hauled off to jail or killed. Any voluntary interaction between any of us is first filtered through the screen of approved actions. Slavery wearing Freedom's clothes.

Ultimately, each person—willingly or not—is the warrior of their own philosophy. Many Americans live with the philosophy that the Earth belongs to us; and so consuming everything within it is a natural extension. Our government, (at least in part) a natural extension of popular opinion, behaves as if the Earth belongs to us, and so ruling everyone is an extension of our self-righteousness. And so with every decision that each person makes, they enforce these ideas or support ideas of their own.

> "Material abundance without character is the path to destruction." -Thomas Jefferson

Each person can only do the best they can, where they are at, with what they have. We each bare the responsibility for doing whatever we can to create the kind of world we want to live in. If you want to live in a healthy world, you have to start making healthy choices. If you want to live in a free world, you have to start rejecting the erosion of liberty. It's really not about "doing" anything, so much as not doing. We need to withdraw our support from monopolies as much as possible; not support them. Pay as little taxes as possible. Trade alternative currencies. Buy as locally as possible. Help your family, friends, and community as much as possible. I won't tell you what to do or not to do, only that you should look at information and make up your own mind. Check out what Monsanto has been up to. Look at how many people die from properly proscribed pills every year. Fluoride seems pretty toxic, should it be in drinking water? (What is now) Conventional food, medicine, and water all seem to have serious health consequences. Whether or not we all agree on the causes and effects, it's healthier for each of us, our communities, and our economies to do everything as local as possible.

It should also be mentioned; I have seen squabbles with various people amongst each other. As individuals, it isn't difficult to understand our common enemy; the cancer that threatens to devour us all. It behooves all people of like-mind to work together, at least until their paths split. Libertarians and Agorists each oppose power in their own way—we are so far away from either's vision—and it would benefit both sides to work toward mutual aims until reality has so caught up with ideals that different roads can be taken. There are so many people interested in liberty...if only they could work together!

And that is one contribution I am hoping to make with this book—especially after seeing the chart—hopefully the economist and the farmer, the school teacher and the police officer, the soldier and the entertainer, the anarchist, the environmentalist, and the libertarian, every family that wants to grow old together, and any person of any peaceful religious belief can all see how we are tricked into enslaving each other. Instead, we can choose to work toward our mutual freedom. *The man willing to initiate violence on other men is an enemy to everyone attempting to live a peaceful life.* When building new ideas, it is easy to diverge, but in resistance to evil and violence it should be easy to unify.

Power corrupts. Is there any argument? Any debate? All of history—real history, not the whitewashed, establishment approved version of heroes—is testament. Not even ten years after signing Free Speech into law, the very same people passed the Alien and Sedition Acts. Power corrupts. Yet, if you turn on the television, you hear dunces like Paul Krugman argue for the increase and centralization of power on a daily basis. Any increase (or centralization) of power is merely an increase and centralization of corruption (if not now, certainly in the future). Advocating for the centralization of power (the power has to come from somewhere; it is taken from the herd) is the same thing as advocating for corruption. What kind of person advocates for corruption? Even a Nobel Prize winner, a supposed intellectual, like Krugman is swept aside by a single paragraph of basic logic (or revealed as a sinister shill).

Let's say you hear a knock on the door in the middle of the night. You open the door; it's a man with a gun, demanding whatever cash you have handy in your wallet. Let's look at a few scenarios. Let's say you beg him to calm down, go get your cash, and thank him for letting you live. Or instead, let's say you tell him you'll be right back with the money, go get a gun and shoot at him as he's standing there waiting. He'll obviously flee, maybe with his life. Or instead you refuse to answer the door? Or slam the door in his face?

In which scenario are you likely to be *robbed a second time*? The point isn't violence. I don't advocate violence against the government (though I don't dissuade anyone from legitimate self-defense either). I only advocate resistance. The slave master getting nothing from his slaves is forced into another venture.

The government doesn't want to just outright murder everyone. You can't make money with a bunch of corpses. It wouldn't do slave owners any good to murder all their slaves; who will work the plantation? They'll resort to violence if they have to, but they'd prefer to uphold the illusions of freedom and nobility, since the slaves work much better (they make more money) in that kind of environment. The government wants productive dairy cows, and so long as we acquiesce, so long as we play the game, we'll continue to get milked.

> "It behooves every man who values liberty of conscience for himself, to resist invasions of it in the case of others" -Thomas Jefferson

One of the most powerful monopolies is the monopoly on school. Indoctrinating young minds is the recipe for future control. Whatever hope there is for freedom in the future will probably be directly correlated with the number of minds that haven't been smashed into retardation and submission. Just as the Internet has been a boon to Freedom (decentralizing information), so any measure to decentralize school is a benefit to every mind involved.

Do you buy your groceries from a local farm? Or do you buy your groceries from a big supermarket? Each purchase at a local farm supports local farmers and healthier food. Each purchase at the grocery store supports big corporations and horrible practices of the agribusiness. When you see somebody who needs help, do you help them or do you just assume somebody else will do something? Every time you feed the homeless (or do any voluntary act of charity), you prove the naysayers of human possibilities wrong. Every time you do nothing (assuming you have the capabilities to help), you leave suffering for somebody else to alleviate.

But the most important point is that it's not so much a doing as it is a not doing. There's many positive things that can be done but contributing to a healthy society can be accomplished as easily as refusing to continue feeding the cancer that is wracking the body of peaceful society. Everyone doesn't have to become an activist (unrecommended), or a farmer, or have to go live in the woods. But it's easy to stop shopping at giant corporations, stop watching mainstream media, and stop cheerleading the current system. Not voting is marginally easier than voting. The eventual success of the parasite probably depends on the willingness of people feed it with their lives.

It's at this point in books where the author extols the reader to get politically active. Get involved in the process. Write your legislators. Work on campaigns. Vote! And I cannot think of a bigger waste of time. Voting is the most ineffectual method for any type of change. I have attempted to demonstrate how many of the problems we face are a direct result of the system; *systematic problems.* Once this is understood, solutions become much clearer; no solution can come from the system. If problems exist *because* of the system, there is no reform, there is no change, there is no fix; the system must be removed for healing to take place. Voting is a clever trick—used by the system—to perpetuate the system forever by absorbing anger and frustration back into the system. The dairy farm is unhealthy for the cows, relative to a natural existence. No dairy farm reform will make the farm as natural as nature itself.

Voting isn't a right, responsibility, or even a duty. Voting is a scam. You can't vote for a representative; only you can represent yourself (just as representatives end up representing themselves and their interests).

Voting gives the illusion that we have done something when nothing has done. Voting gives the illusion that something has been created when it has not.

Worse, voting gives consent. When all the politicians claiming to represent people do whatever they want, they claim to have the "consent" of the people they represent. Meaning, they have been voted for. If everyone who had a legitimate complaint with the monopolies abstained from voting (which should be everyone, since we're all being fleeced by the government and banking cartels) they would either have to show their true nature or go home.

Elections are merely stepping stones to tyranny, destruction, and death because no election can change Natural laws. *No vote can change principles.* Is there a functioning human mind on the planet that would argue that a vote would change gravity? Is murder any different? Can a vote change murder? Obviously not, so what then is the value of voting?

If the system is based on illegitimate principles, every action in affirmation of the system reinforces the illusion of legitimacy. Voting, change, reform; illusory cheese! A vote only keeps the system going, it doesn't change anything. A vote encourages slavery, extortion, theft, and murder.

There is no value in voting. It is only an expression of consent. If you consent to be a slave, your vote will make your masters feel justified in living at your expense.

I often hear the lament "If only we got the right people into office.." Aside from the fact (yes, the fact) that this has never happened in at least the last 200 years (the founders get a pass, since they bled and died to create their own system, more than we can say..) of our history (has it happened anywhere?), the sentiment betrays an ignorant, hypocritical view of the world. The "right people" are obviously the people who would do whatever it is that the speaker would want. A dictatorship could be a beautiful form of government...if your best friend is the dictator. Monarchy is sweet...if you're the king.

We've been conditioned for all of our lives to believe that our system of monopolies is the greatest, freest, most holiest system that has ever existed in the history of anything that will ever exist. There's certainly some merit to the argument when held relative to other countries; but in a comparison of turds *you're still comparing turds!* One turd being less stinky doesn't make it filet mignon, it makes it less stinky.

You and I cannot simultaneously be free and slaves. We're either making our own choices, or we are not. We are either doing as we are told, or we are not. We are either free individuals or property of the owners. Which is it? Anyone who claims—here and now—that we are free individuals is being intellectually dishonest.

And so the true nature, and true evil, of monopolies is revealed. Monopolies create masters and slaves. You can see in the chart how one monopoly leads to another, but the truth stands plainly for anyone to see. The true nature of our government is that each person is now given two choices: make the rules on somebody else or have the rules made on you. You become the master or you become the slave.

Getting the "right people" into office assumes that the "wrong people" have been in office. There is no right person for the office of determining which American citizens should be assassinated (as Obama now does). Citizens should never be assassinated. There is no right person for the office of deciding which countries we are gong to invade and loot. We should not be aggressors. There is no right person for the office of determining who should get taxed and where the money should go. Nobody should be robbed. Nobody should receive stolen property.

Getting the "right people" into office assumes that there should be an office in the first place...what kind of cow wants to live in a world of dairy farmers?

It should also be pointed out that there are millions of people who currently make decisions of governance and law; from the president to the local judge. There is *no possible way,* logistically, to sift through all the decisions and separate the good ones from the bad ones. *We will be dead before can even know what has happened, let alone consider the implications.* Sure, sometimes something positive could happen, but how often? And how are we supposed to figure it out, covered up by classification, obfuscation, and buried within a tomb of bureaucracy that few things escape? If we can understand an illegitimate principle when we see one, no nitpicking is necessary. It is literally impossible for anyone to go through the scope of government and law and pick out the good and the bad, and for society to move in that direction. Therefore, the only rational choice left for anyone of good conscious is a wholesale resistance of the system that allows evil to perpetuate on such a large magnitude; resisting *all* monopolies.

Another oft-heard lament, "What we *really* need is a return to the Constitution." I certainly agree with the sentiment and any move in that direction is preferable. However, this line of thinking betrays a naivety and ignorance of history and governance.

The Constitution was ignored, starting with the Alien and Sedition Acts. It continued with countless illegitimate wars, broken treaties, central banks, and let's not forget outright slavery (I'm assuming the sentiment doesn't urge a return to that), right up until Abraham Lincoln discarded the Constitution in the Civil War. (According to the 10th Amendment, States have sovereignty over the Federal Government in all issues not mentioned in the

Constitution. They could peacefully withdraw if they chose to, which they did, and half a million people were slaughtered to bring them back into line. Sound Constitutional?) Since then, despotism is merely coasting into place.

If 200+ years of the Constitution got us into this mess, why would a return to the Constitution not end up right here again? What would a "return to the Constitution" prevent a second time that it missed the first? Lysander Spooner intellectually blew this argument away—150 years ago—with two sentences:

> "But whether the Constitution really be one thing, or another, this much is certain - that it has either authorized such a government as we have had, or has been powerless to prevent it. In either case, it is unfit to exist."

A "return to the Constitution" also begs a complete ignorance of history and logic. How can there be a return to anything in a completely different manner than the thing was established in the first place? Is there a return to a healthier environment by changing or reducing pollution and destruction? Obviously not, a return to a healthier environment would the cessation of pollution and destruction. Likewise, was the Constitution established through blogging, bumper stickers, writing representatives, and voting for Presidents? Obviously not, so how would a "return" to the Constitution be effected by those means? It's complete nonsense.

But I can tell you that those in power seem to understand what a "return to the Constitution" would mean, and if it could be accomplished with blogging, voting, and flag-waving, those would be illegal. Or is it just a coincidence that the Bill of Rights is continually, narrowly redefined? Is it a coincidence that domestic police are being militarized? Is it a coincidence that government surveillance is on a tremendous rise? Is it a coincidence that private citizens have had their choice in arms diminished while local police buy armored vehicles and sniper rifles? Is it a coincidence that the NSA is building a giant database to screen every email, telephone call, and text message sent in the country? Is it a coincidence that the Department of *Homeland Security* is buying *hundreds of millions* of lethal rounds of ammunition? Are these just random coincidences? Do these seem like logical steps that a farmer would take if he saw the herd becoming unproductive and restless? Or are they merely happenstance?

I do not advocate violence against the government, or anyone else for that matter. Our government is the most effective machine of destruction ever seen in the history of the planet. As far as the system is concerned, it doesn't matter whether we fight it or not; it is about to fail, crushing millions underneath. The only question is whether it will be succeeded by something better or not. A ponzi scheme of monopolies, unlimited growth, and slavery is coming to an end; will a similar one replace it? Or will we begin building the kinds of communities we want to live in now? Life is a series of choices; there is no non-choice. Refusing to choose is refusing to live. And so monopolies float onward through the unwilling choices of the ignorant and apathetic.

We don't need a violent revolution. We don't need to be at war with governments or laws. Wars for the future are wars against ignorance. Wars of the future are wars against apathy; will people suffer themselves to be peasants? Or will they become so passionately aware of the life they have been blessed with that they are determined not to let some fool with a degree, badge, or flag waste it?

We need a revolution in the minds and hearts of men and women. We need the courage to look outside the fence, look into the wilderness, and to imagine the possibilities.

We need the understanding that we cannot live apart from the planet; a poisoned environment will lead to poisoned people.

Each person can only do what they can. Every step toward your own improvement, your own self-reliance, your own independence, is a step toward the health and prosperity of your family and your community. Principled living is the antithesis of the ignorant, compliant, obedience of the slave. And principled living requires nothing but desire.

We don't need a return to the Constitution. We don't even need a new Constitution. We need a generation of men and women who are willing to create their own free society. We don't need more pieces of paper for legislators to pay lip service to while stealing and murdering. We need a generation of men and women who are not going to sit quietly for theft, murder, and slavery. We need a generation of men and women who are willing to look inside of themselves, realize their own potential and birthright, and sign the Constitution of a Free Mind, Body, and Soul. We need a generation of men and women to sign a Declaration of Independence with their actions from the monopolies enslaving the world; willing to live and act peacefully amongst each other.

Lord Byron wrote:

> Or tear their name defil'd from Slavery's mournful page
> Hereditary bondsman, know ye not
> Who would be free themselves must strike the blow?

Elisabeth Kubler-Ross explained the five stages of grief in her book "On Death and Dying". The book was about her work with terminally ill patients but it might as well be a work on terminally ill civilizations. However, notice that none of the following stages of grief are helpful to the patient, except for the last one. Only at the end can the patient make a decision with reality in mind.

The first stage of grief is *denial.* This could never happen to us! We imagine ourselves as the (holy) empire (see: superpower) that can never fall. It'll never happen here. There's bad guys all over the planet, but not in a country governed by such a noble document as ours. It can't happen in a country that is so rich...so rich as long as you have absolutely no understanding of economics. Being kept busy in ignorance and denial is the easiest way to never progress.

The next three stages of grief are *anger, bargaining,* and *depression.* People who are active in politics display all three traits. Many are angry. (Angry at the other party, those heartless jerks!) Many are frustrated. Many are exasperated. And many imagine they can still bargain. Change the system. Reform the system. Get the right people in office...and on and on and on.

The last stage is *acceptance.* Only then can the grieving face reality and make pertinent decisions. It would go without my pointing out, the longer a person remains in one of the first four stages, the longer it takes them to *actually address reality.* All the denial, anger, bargaining, and depression in the world does not change the reality. The longer it takes to move on to real solutions. Ignorance, denial, perceptions, illusory cheese, sentimental investment, division, diversification, the manipulation of words, minds, and emotions are all *designed* to keep people away from *acceptance.* Acceptance that an evil exists, it exists within our midst, and it must be addressed.

Freedom doesn't come from governments. Freedom doesn't come from the military. Freedom doesn't come from money or pieces of paper with rules or grades on them. As a society is ultimately made up of individuals, Freedom is the natural right of each individual in the society. Freedom is the God-given, equal right of each man and woman; and with Freedom comes responsibility and consequence.

The condition of the dairy farm affects every cow. The condition of the plantation is in the interest of every slave. So long as the majority of people are in denial about the reality that faces them, they will be slaves. Ignorance is required for subservience. So long as the majority of people are angry, try to reform the system, or slide into depression and apathy, they will be slaves. Only when they accept reality, take responsibility for themselves, do whatever they can, where they are at, with what they have; only then will they be free.

I understand that people are busy. These seem like lofty ideas; lofty goals. Most people are just trying to put food on the table, or forget about a crappy job, or struggling with some personal issue. We are lonely; possibly the loneliest society the planet has ever seen, zoned into televisions and cell phones. Most people are just trying to get by. I understand, and I sympathize.

Many people simply cannot think about anything other than the current struggle; I've been there. When I am sick, all I can think about is getting healthy. When I am poor, all I can think about is working, or more ways to make money. When I am hungry, all I can think about is eating. I understand the singlemindedness that suffering creates.

However, it's important to understand that much of the suffering experienced in the world today is a direct result of living on a plantation. Much of the hunger, sickness, poverty, anger, and violence is a *direct result* of living in a civilization of monopolized cartels dictating when who gets what. Much of the suffering we witness now will never be alleviated until the boot of monopolies is removed from the neck of humanity.

I have heard it said that we are entering a new age; The Information Age. I agree we are entering a new age, but it is not one of Information. We are entering the Age of The Institution.

In a global world, violence is institutionalized; governments, laws, coalitions, treaties, sanctions, and wars. And so the dominance of The Institution in every aspect of life is only a natural following.

Just a few hundred years ago, a variety of societies existed outside the boundaries of what would now be called the "western world". Through colonialization and dominance, the unlimited growth required by constantly stealing from the next man was supplied at the expense of other cultures, but what happens when all the land is taken? What happens to a ponzi scheme when capacity has been reached?

So the slave owners are buckling down, getting ready for leaner times on the plantation; there is no more low hanging fruit. Stricter controls, tighter work schedule, and extreme conformity.

A generation ago it was possible to travel without papers, every digital correspondence wasn't recorded by secret police organizations, and the lack of a college diploma wasn't viewed as a professional death sentence. We have become far removed from our natural environment; people used to grow some of their own food. Food is now manufactured with a combination of chemical companies and giant monoculture agrofarms. Medicine consists of pills, made by more chemical companies. Entering into society consists of the standard path of submitting oneself to the institution of school to get the diploma to work at the good company for the good retirement. Every aspect of life consists of submitting to the ever larger institution of government; all a result of the institutionalization of violence.

While the sickness hasn't completely spread to the rest of the world, look at how the mind works in The United States. Food must be approved by the Institution. Medicine must be approved by the Institution. Businesses and their transactions must be approved by the Institution. News comes from the Institution. Popular commodities in the marketplace (movies, music, art, sports) spend massive budgets marketing themselves as having come from the Institution (a big label, big studio, official league, official sponsor).

The Institution requires certification for the smallest actions. You think you can just live on this planet? Think again. Papers please! A birth certificate. Social Security Card. Medical record. Proof of insurance. Degree. Diploma. Passport. Register your vehicle. Proof of insurance. Get a license to operate the vehicle. License to marry. Proof of insurance. Get a receipt with the big screen television. License to start a business. Proof of insurance. License to sell cars. License to sell real estate. Get a receipt with the donut. License to practice law. License to practice medicine. Proof of insurance. Certificate to give nutritional advice. License to sell food. And finally, a death certificate (and proof of insurance).

The Institution is a diversified rebirth of despotism; all that is official; all that is uniform; total conformity. The Institution has the broadest and basest solutions for everyone but those at the top; minimum subsistence and maximum production. The Institution is streamlining the planet into commodities, into one giant plantation; the masters and slaves. Government and law need have no concern for religions, government and law *are* the new religion. The Church of the State counts among its most fervent worshipers many supposed members of Christianity and Islam.

The Institution is spreading its tendrils across the face of the planet; faster every second. George Orwell's horrific vision in 1984 is now almost our reality. The Institution, and all that it stands for—violence, control, compliance, obedience, conformity, security, compromise, slavery, and death—is the antithesis of humanity, and everything good in the natural world; peace, prosperity, freedom, happiness, creativity, ingenuity, spontaneity, charity, understanding, diversity, and life. In all of it's many forms—from the institution of school to the institution of violence—The Institution is the enemy of life. The Institution is the enemy of nature. *The institution is the enemy of humanity.*

There is no half-way. There is no partial bits of a pseudo-institutionalized solution. Everyone cannot be a slave master, but the Institution will always have an open position for the willing bootlicker. The Institution is steamrolling forward to stamp out the uniqueness in the world, replacing it with nothing more than a plantation; where you will be "free" to live so long as you have filled out the necessary paperwork and march in step with whatever the heads of the Institution deem acceptable.

Make no mistake, security is an illusion. There will be bloodshed either way. Masses are butchered within governments just as easily without. Easier, in fact. There is no easy choice. There is only the Institution of Slavery, or a free, natural, voluntary, peaceful attempt at life. Will we embrace a lifetime of slavery? Will we thank God, or our benevolent landlords, for the privilege and security of living hand-to-mouth for the benefit of our superiors?

Or will we demonstrate with our lives a refusal to be managed and the willingness to live productively, as equals with our neighbors?

This book is available on Amazon.com in paperback and Kindle formats. An .mp3 audiobook will be forthcoming, available for purchase through my website.

There's no million dollar budgets or marketing teams behind this book. This book is self-published. If you've enjoyed the book, please spread the word. You can see some of my art and the manifestations of my ideas at my website www.EndlessUnlimited.com.

If you've gotten the book for free and it's added value to your life, please donate via the website. Books don't write themselves.

RECOMMENDED READING

(a few authors/books that have strongly impacted me)

"A People's History of the United States" by Howard Zinn
Anything written by Ralph Waldo Emerson
"Civil Disobedience" "Life Without Principles" and "Walden" by Thoreau
"1984" by George Orwell
"The Republic" by Plato
"Think and Grow Rich" by Napolean Hill
"The Art of War" Sun Tzu
"The Alchemist" and "The Pilgrimage" by Paulo Coelho
"The Fountainhead" and "Atlas Shrugged" by Ayn Rand
"The Tao of Jeet Kune Do" by Bruce Lee
"End The Fed" by Ron Paul
"Nullification" by Tom Woods
"Ishmael" by Daniel Quinn
"The War of Art" by Steven Pressfield
"Rollback" by Thomas E Woods Jr.
"The Book of Five Rings" by Miyamoto Musashi
"Blankets" by Craig Thompson
"Great Expectations" by Charles Dickens
"Family and Civilization" by Carle Zimmerman
"Blink" by Malcolm Gladwell
"Teach like Your Hair's on Fire" by Rafe Esquith
"Blue Like Jazz" by Don Miller
"Peaceful Mind" John R. McQuaid et al
Any essay by William Norman Grigg
LewRockwell.com
The Bible

--a more comprehensive list of books and websites is available on my website.

ABOUT THE AUTHOR

I am a scholar in the tradition of Emerson; and a philosopher, writer, and artist from Seattle, Washington. I love a good conversation, a good sunset, and a competitive game of anything; ultimate frisbee, dodgeball, or tactical board games in particular. I've been to more than my share of school (unfortunately). I've come to the conclusion that almost everything useful I now know, I never learned in school. I am always listening to music. I am infinitely curious; an unending question-asker. I am always thinking, especially in the shower. If I go too long without reading, my mind feels as if it is rotting away.

One of my all-time favorite lyrics:

The fans is watchin',
Nigga's plottin' to get me,
Will I survive? Will I die?
Come on, let's picture the possibilities.

Currently listening: Grieves, Blue Scholars, Mattson 2.
Favorite Movies: Ping Pong (Japan 2001), The Constant Gardener, Adaptation, The Prestige, Watchmen.

I am available for speaking appearances or interviews on your show, along the lines of philosophy, psychology, and politics. To discuss your project, please email me michael@endlessunlimited.com.

In the tradition of Courage Wolf, I keep the door open for all challengers, feel free to shoot me an email if you have any comments, suggestions, constructive criticisms, clever stories, or good jokes.

58750145R00101

Made in the USA
Lexington, KY
16 December 2016